BURLINGTON
NORTHERN SANTA FE
═ RAILWAY HERITAGE ═

Santa Fe Railway 3,000-horsepower passenger hauling diesel electric locomotive No. 404 (one of six, Nos. 400–405, type U30CG delivered in November 1967 by General Electric Company [GE]), is heading the passenger train "Tulsan" at Iola, a city and county seat of Allen County, Kansas. The Tulsan connected Tulsa, Oklahoma, with Kansas City, Missouri. On December 10, 1939, the Tulsan was predominantly equipped with light weight stainless steel equipment built by the Budd Company. With declining ridership dining service was removed on April 1, 1963. The Tulsan made its final run on April 30, 1971. The U30CG locomotives were later renumbered 8000–8005, repainted blue and yellow, and were mainly used in freight service until September 22, 1980 when they were traded into GE for new locomotives. (*Photographer Mac Owen Used with permission from Audio-Visual Designs [www.audiovisualdesigns.com]*)

Four Burlington Northern Railroad 3,000-horsepower type SD40-2 locomotives (built by the Electro-Motive Division of General Motors [EMD]) headed by No. 7052 are powering a train of Montana and Wyoming coal that will be used for a power plant that is a major source of power for Madison, the state capital of Wisconsin. The SD40-2 locomotive, with a modular electronic control system, was an improvement over the SD40. (*Photographer Rod Kreunen Used with permission from Audio-Visual Designs [www.audiovisualdesigns.com]*)

BURLINGTON
NORTHERN SANTA FE
═ RAILWAY HERITAGE ═

Beth Anne Keates and Kenneth C. Springirth

AMERICA
THROUGH TIME®
ADDING COLOR TO AMERICAN HISTORY

Atchison, Topeka & Santa Fe Railway gas electric car (commonly called a Doodlebug) No. M160, built by Brill in June 1931, initially handled service between Kansas and Texas. In the 1960s, this car provided service between Clovis and Carlsbad, New Mexico. It was placed on display at the Age of Steam Railroad Museum in Dallas and later at the Museum of the American Railroad in Frisco, Texas. (*Photographer E.W. Anderson Used with permission from Audio-Visual Designs [www.audiovisualdesigns.com]*)

On top portion of cover: On April 3, 2022, Burlington Northern Santa Fe (BNSF) Railway 4,400-horsepower locomotive No. 6017 (GE type ES44AC built in June 2006) is at the North Yard in the city of Saginaw, in Tarrant County, Texas. This locomotive, weighing 420,000 pounds and having a top speed of 73 miles per hour, commemorated the twenty-fifth anniversary of the December 31, 1996 merger of the Atchison, Topeka & Santa Fe Railway with the Burlington Northern Railroad creating the Burlington Northern Santa Fe Railway. (*Dylan Chastain photograph*)

On bottom portion of front cover: Atchison, Topeka & Santa Fe Railway (AT&SF) six-axle diesel electric locomotive No. 5700 (3,600-horsepower type SD45-2 built by EMD in May 1973) is awaiting the next assignment. The SD45-2 was an improved version of the EMD SD45. This was the first of five type SD45-2 locomotives repainted in the United States Bicentennial white and blue paint scheme. (*Santa Fe Railway Used with permission from Audio-Visual Designs [www.audiovisualdesigns.com]*)

Back cover: Santa Fe 1,500-horsepower type F7A diesel electric locomotive No. 338 (built in May 1953 by EMD promoted originally as a freight locomotive but was also used in passenger service) is heading five diesel units ready to depart Joliet, Illinois, for a trip to the western United States. There is a good possibility that this train is the *San Francisco Chief* which according to the June 6, 1954 Official Guide left Chicago at 12:20 p.m., made a flag stop at Joliet, and in two days accumulating 2,554.7 miles arrived at Oakland at 11:25 a.m. (*Photographer Owen Leander Used with permission from Audio-Visual Designs [www.audiovisualdesigns.com]*)

America Through Time is an imprint of Fonthill Media LLC
www.through-time.com | office@through-time.com

First published 2023

Copyright © Beth Anne Keates and Kenneth C. Springirth 2023

ISBN 978-1-63499-448-4

Typeset in Mrs Eaves XL Serif Narrow
Printed and bound in England

Published by Arcadia Publishing by arrangement with Fonthill Media LLC
For all general information, please contact Arcadia Publishing:

Telephone: 843-853-2070
Fax: 843-853-0044
E-mail: sales@arcadiapublishing.com
For customer service and orders:
Toll-Free 1-888-313-2665

www.arcadiapublishing.com

Contents

Acknowledgments

Thanks to the Erie County (Pennsylvania) Public Library system for their inter-library loan system. Dylan Chastain, Bob Elder, Andrew L. Keates, Beth Anne Keates, Brian A. Keates, Doug Lacey, and Edwin Wilde provided photographs. A number of pictures came from postcards and were (*Used with permission from Audio-Visual Designs [www.audiovisualdesigns.com]*). The names of the photographers who took the pictures for those postcards are as follows: E. W. Anderson, John D. Bartley, Leo Caloia, D. Christensen, Ken Crist, Don Erb, Ed Fulcomer, Lewis A. Harlow, W. L. Heitter, Rod Kreunen, Owen Leander, Mac Owen, Russ Porter, Jim Shaughnessy, Donald E. Smith, and J. W. Swanberg. Burlington Northern Santa Fe Railway website www.bnsf.com, Form 10-K Reports, Eno Center for Transportation, Commuter Rail Division of the Regional Transportation Authority and the Northeast Illinois Regional Commuter Railroad Corporation Management's Discussion and Analysis December 31, 2020 plus Metra Ridership Trends 2021 Annual Report (Updated March 2022) were important information sources. Books that served as excellent reference sources were: *BNSF Railway Locomotive Directory 2019–2020* by Paul Wester and Paul K. Withers, *Early History of Gallitzin* by F. J. Parrish, *Everywhere West The Burlington Route* by Patrick C. Dorn, *Norfolk Southern Locomotive Directory 2017–2018* by Paul K. Withers, *Santa Fe Railway* by Steve Glishinski, *Souvenir of the Chicago, Burlington & Quincy Railroad and Associated Lines* published 1933, and *The Burlington in Transition* by Bernard G. Corbin and Joseph C. Hardy.

This book is dedicated to co-author Kenneth C. Springirth's son Philip Thomas Springirth, for his brilliance in solving challenges in this high-tech world.

Santa Fe 2,000-horsepower passenger diesel locomotive No. 11, type E3A built in August 1939 by Electro Motive Corporation (EMC), is at Dallas, Texas. Compared with passenger locomotives made later by EMD, type E3 locomotives made by EMC had a more pronounced slant when viewed from the side. (*Photographer Mac Owen Used with permission from Audio-Visual Designs [www.audiovisualdesigns.com]*)

Introduction

The History of the Burlington Northern Santa Fe Railway began with the chartering of the Aurora Branch Railroad by the October 2, 1848 Act of the Illinois General Assembly. The Aurora Branch Railroad was built in Illinois from Aurora via Naperville, Lisle, Downers Grove, Hinsdale, and Berwyn to the west side of Chicago. This became the Chicago and Aurora Railroad in 1852 and Chicago, Burlington & Quincy Railroad (CB&Q) in 1856. Of the 204 railroads that became part of the CB&Q, the Hannibal & St. Joseph Railroad, completed in 1859, brought mail across Missouri to connect with the Pony Express and introduced the first railcar equipped for sorting U.S. mail *en route* in 1862. The CB&Q purchased the Colorado & Southern plus Fort Worth & Denver Railways in 1908 giving it access south to Dallas, Houston, and Galveston. In 1925, the CB&Q purchased a gas electric car from the Brill Company. By 1930, the CB&Q operated fifty gas-electric cars plus seven gas-mechanical cars. These cars had an excellent operating record with 94 percent availability and reduced expenses 36.3 percent over steam passenger service. The use of these cars ended around 1961. Beginning April 9, 1929, buses replaced an unprofitable passenger train service between Lincoln and Omaha. By 1930, the CB&Q grossed $305,000 on its bus operations and at the same time saved $114,367 by eliminating unprofitable lightly travelled local trains. The chief advantage of the bus service was to reduce the excessive costs of the unprofitable local service and improve the profitability of the remaining passenger train service. In the *Souvenir of the Chicago, Burlington & Quincy Railroad and Associated Lines* published in 1933, the Burlington noted: "It never defaulted on its interest charges and no mortgage upon it was ever foreclosed. It went through the Civil War and the Panics of 1873, 1893, 1907, and through the Depression of 1930–33, but it never was in the hands of a receiver." On May 26, 1934, the CB&Q introduced the Budd Company-built *Zephyr*, the first United States streamlined stainless steel permanently articulated passenger trainset powered by a Winton 201A diesel engine, which made a special 1,015.4-mile non-stop run from Denver, Colorado, to Chicago, Illinois, in thirteen hours and five minutes at an average speed of almost 78 miles per hour with the highest speed attained of 112.5 miles per hour setting a new long-distance speed record. This train was placed in regular service on November 11, 1934 between Lincoln and Omaha, Nebraska, and Kansas City, Missouri. As noted in *Everywhere West: The Burlington Route* by Patrick C. Dorin: "As 1934 turned to 1935, the *Zephyr* began to do its stuff for which it was intended. The average cost per mile was 4.22 cents per mile as compared to 5.08 cents for steam for general maintenance.

The overall total costs were 34.21 cents per mile for the *Zephyr* as compared to 63.75 cents for steam." Reducing costs and initially attracting passengers, this *Zephyr* operated until retirement in 1960, and was donated to the Chicago, Illinois, Museum of Science & Industry. In 1945, the CB&Q introduced the first United States vista dome car, and in 1952 became the first railroad to completely dieselize a suburban service. The last new *Zephyr* (*Denver Zephyr*) went into service in 1956 with three vista dome cars. This train showed CB&Q's faith in passenger service when most railroads faced declining ridership due to the automobile and government subsidizing air and bus service. By the mid-1960s as the interstate highway system neared completion and rail post office cars were withdrawn, all of the *Zephyrs* were discontinued by 1970. The CB&Q merged with the Great Northern, Northern Pacific, and Spokane, Portland & Seattle Railway on March 2, 1970 to form the Burlington Northern Railroad. On December 31, 1996, the Burlington Northern Railroad acquired the Atchison, Topeka & Santa Fe Railway and became Burlington Northern Santa Fe Railway that was later renamed BNSF Railway which was owned by the Burlington Northern Santa Fe Corporation. Berkshire Hathaway, controlled by investor Warren Buffet, purchased that corporation in 2009.

The Colorado & Southern Railway (C&SR) was chartered in Colorado on December 19, 1898. It formed on January 11, 1899 by acquiring the Union Pacific, Denver & Gulf Company plus the Denver, Leadville & Gunnison Railway Company, both of which were former subsidiaries of the Union Pacific. Added to the C&SR by 1910 were Fort Worth & Denver City Railway, Wichita Valley Railroad, Wichita Valley Railway, Abilene & Northern Railway, Stamford & Northwestern Railway, Fort Worth & Denver Terminal Railway, Wichita Falls & Oklahoma Railway, and a 50 percent interest in the Trinity & Brazos Valley Railway. The CB&Q purchased the Colorado & Southern Railway (C&SR) in December 1908; however, the C&SR continued to operate as a separate company and was merged into the Burlington Northern Railroad on December 31, 1981.

The Fort Worth & Denver City Railway (FW&DCR), chartered by the Texas Legislature on May 26, 1873, was the first railroad line to penetrate the northwest part of Texas and contributed to the growth of Texas cities such as Wichita Falls and Amarillo. In addition, the FW&DCR promoted the rural areas it served by providing free seeds, trees, and tree seedlings to farmers and ranchers to encourage cotton growing, wheat growing, and reduce soil erosion. On August 7, 1951, the railroad changed its name to the Fort Worth & Denver Railway (FW&D). The Burlington Northern

Railroad (BN) acquired the FW&D by virtue of the BN and Colorado Southern merger on December 31, 1981. FW&D corporate existence ended when it was formally merged into the Burlington Northern Railroad on December 31, 1982.

The Atchison, Topeka & Santa Fe Railroad (AT&SF) was chartered in February 1859 to serve the cities of Atchison and Topeka in Kansas and Santa Fe, New Mexico, and became known as the Santa Fe. In 1868, the United States Congress authorized the AT&SF to purchase unallotted lands of the Pottawattomie Indian Reservation near Topeka, Kansas, for $1 an acre. The AT&SF resold the land to farmers which provided the necessary funding to begin construction of the railroad on Washington Street between Fourth and Fifth Street in Topeka, Kansas, on October 30, 1868. Santa Fe's first locomotive (named after Cyrus K. Holiday who had made a fortune in railroad construction and had the idea to build a railroad to bring prosperity to Topeka and surrounding area) on April 26, 1869, pulled the first AT&SF train from Topeka, 7 miles west of Wakarusa. The railroad was completed to Newton, Kansas, in July 1871; reached Atchison on May 16, 1872; and on December 28, 1872 reached the Kansas–Colorado border; and Pueblo, Colorado, on February 29, 1876. Initially, the AT&SF bypassed Santa Fe because of the engineering challenges of the mountainous terrain. Later a branch line was built from Lamy, New Mexico, to Santa Fe. The Santa Fe set up real estate offices and sold farmland from the land grants that the railroad was awarded by the United States Congress. These new farms would create a need for freight and passenger service. More than 8,000 Russian-born Mennonites migrated to an area near Newton, Kansas. Despite disaster from drought and grasshoppers, the Mennonites raised crops in what had been desolate land. The hard red wheat seed they brought with them helped make Kansas the United States' breadbasket. Building westward, it reached San Diego and Los Angeles by 1887, eastward reached Chicago in 1887, and Amarillo, Texas, in 1887. By 1889, the Santa Fe routes reached Chicago, Galveston, Los Angeles, and San Diego. As economic conditions deteriorated, the railroad went bankrupt in 1893. A new company Atchison, Topeka & Santa Fe Railway purchased Santa Fe's assets out of receivership in 1895. In 1900, the Santa Fe completed a line from Stockton to Richmond, California. Through the purchase and rebuilding of another railroad, Santa Fe acquired its own route from Richmond to Oakland, California, which gave Santa Fe control of its own routes from Chicago to Los Angeles, San Diego, the Bay Area, and into Texas. Santa Fe passenger service set a standard for quality and attention to detail with famous trains such as the Super Chief and El Capitan. Its passenger service ended when Amtrak took over United States passenger service on May 1, 1971. Numerous branch lines were added by nominally independent companies that became part of AT&SF. Its approximately 1,500 miles of oil lines connected many oil fields with the outside world. Much of the Santa Fe's success was a result of its willingness to strive for excellence. Santa Fe's peak mileage of 13,568 was reached in 1931. During World War II, Santa Fe's passenger traffic rose 88 percent between 1941 and 1942, and the amount of freight moved almost doubled. In the 1960s, freight service operated at faster speeds and truck trailers became a common sight on the Santa Fe. During the 1980s, new labor agreements reduced the number of crew in a train to two, eliminated cabooses, and allowed crews to operate through several crew change points. The Atchison, Topeka & Santa Fe Railway merged into the Burlington Northern Railroad on December 31, 1996 with the new railroad named Burlington Northern Santa Fe Railway.

The Toledo, Peoria & Warsaw Railway opened in 1868 from the Indiana state line across Illinois to the Mississippi River at Warsaw. It was reorganized as the Toledo, Peoria & Western Railroad in 1880 and was leased by the Wabash, St. Louis & Pacific Railway. That lease lasted four years, after which it was taken over by the Toledo, Peoria & Western Railway (TP&W). In 1918, the TP&W affiliated with the Pennsylvania Railroad (PRR). In January 1960, the ATSF and PRR each acquired a 50 percent interest in the TP&W. In 1979, the ATSF acquired the PRR's interest in the TP&W. On December 31, 1983, the TP&W was merged into ATSF. New investors purchased the Lomax–Peoria–Logansport line from ATSF on February 3, 1989 and renamed it TP&W. RailAmerica acquired the line in September 1999 and kept the name TP&W. Genesee & Wyoming acquired RailAmerica in 2012 gaining ownership of the TP&W.

The Alabama, Tennessee & Northern Railroad had its origin when the Mobile & Ohio Railroad chose to build a line in 1897 through Pickens County, Alabama, by way of the town of Reform, Alabama. However, Carrolton, the county seat of Pickens County, wanted a railroad connection to Reform, Alabama, which resulted in the completion of the Carrolton Short Line Railway in 1900. These two railroads eventually combined under the name of the Alabama, Tennessee & Northern Railroad (AT&N) which completed a line from Reform, Alabama, to Mobile, Alabama. By 1948, the St. Louis–San Francisco Railway purchased a controlling interest in the AT&N and operated it as a separate entity until absorbing it in 1971.

The St. Louis–San Francisco Railway (SL&SF) was formed from the Missouri Division and Central Division of the Atlantic & Pacific Railroad (A&P), and was incorporated in Missouri on September 7, 1876. The Atchison, Topeka & Santa Fe Railroad (AT&SF), interested in the A&P right of way, acquired the SL&SF. However the AT&SF had over extended itself and went bankrupt and into receivership in 1893. AT&SF reorganized by 1896 and had to give up control of the SL&SF. The SL&SF had two main lines: St. Louis–Tulsa–Oklahoma City–Floydada, Texas, and Kansas City–Memphis–Birmingham. These two lines crossed in Springfield, Missouri, where the railroad's main shop facility and headquarters were located. On February 28, 1952, the SL&SF operated its last steam locomotive making it the first major railroad to become 100 percent diesel powered. The SL&SF merged into the Burlington Northern on November 21, 1980.

The Great Northern Railway was built in stages by nineteenth-century railroad entrepreneur James J. Hill. Running from

Saint Paul, Minnesota, to Seattle, Washington, it became the northernmost transcontinental railroad route in the United States. On February 1, 1890, Hill consolidated his ownership of railroads into the Great Northern Railway (GNR). The railroad had branches north to the United States–Canada border in Minnesota, North Dakota, and Montana plus branches to Superior, Wisconsin, and Butte, Montana, connecting with the iron range of Minnesota and copper mines in Montana. Hill purchased large parts of the Messabe Iron Range in Minnesota plus its rail lines, and the GNR began shipping iron ore to the Midwest steel mills. The GNR mainline crossed the continental divide through Marias Pass where the mainline is the southern border of Glacier National Park. GNR constructed stations at the East Glacier and West Glacier entrances to the park plus additional inns and lodges in the park. The GNR promoted settlement along its lines in North Dakota and Montana. Receiving no land grants, the GNR purchased land from the federal government, and that land was resold to farmers. The GNR had agencies in Germany and Scandinavia that promoted the railroad's land. Families were transported to the United States where special low cost train cars were built to transport immigrant families. During World War II, the GNR sponsored the 704th Grand Army Division plus the 732nd Railroad Operating Battalion whose officers were previous GNR employees. On March 2, 1970, the Great Northern Railroad along with the Northern Pacific Railway; Chicago, Burlington & Quincy Railroad; and the Spokane, Portland & Seattle Railway merged into the Burlington Northern Railroad which in 1996 merged with the Atchison. Topeka & Santa Fe Railway forming the Burlington Northern Santa Fe Railway.

The Northern Pacific Railway (NPR) operated across the northern part of the western United States from Minnesota to the Pacific Northwest. It was given almost 40 million acres of land grants which it used to raise money for construction. On February 15, 1870, groundbreaking took place at Carlton, Minnesota, and construction crews labored through swamps, bogs, and forests. Construction also began in the west from Kalama, Washington Territory, on the Columbia River near Portland, Oregon. The NPR reached Fargo, Dakota Territory (now North Dakota), in June 1872 and in June 1873 reached Edwinton (now Bismarck), Dakota. In 1866, the NPR completed 164 miles of main line track in North Dakota plus 45 miles in Washington. The NPR reached Dakota Territory at Fargo in 1872. Most of the settlers were German and Scandinavian immigrants who bought the land cheaply, shipped huge amounts of wheat to Minneapolis, and purchased all types of equipment and home supplies that were shipped by rail. On December 16, 1873, the first NPR train arrived at Tacoma, Washington. NPR went into bankruptcy on June 30, 1875, and a reorganization plan was put into effect. Henry Villard, who had

been building an empire of river and water transportation in Oregon, raised $8 million from his associates, purchased control of the NPR, and became president of the NPR on September 15, 1881. Construction crews laid an average of 1.5 miles of track each day, and the Golden Spike was driven near Gold Creek in western Montana on September 8, 1883. As a result of NPR expansion, Northwest Territories in less than seven years had sufficient population to join the Union. North Dakota and South Dakota achieved statehood on November 2, 1889; Montana on November 8, 1889; Washington on November 11, 1889; and Idaho on July 3, 1890. Completion of a 9,850-foot tunnel under Stampede Pass made it possible for the first train to travel directly to Puget Sound. On October 20, 1893, the NPR went into its second bankruptcy. After 1900, the NPR gained access to Chicago, the central Middle West and Texas. When Louis W. Menk became president of the NPR, it was consolidated with the Chicago, Burlington & Quincy Railroad, the Great Northern Railway, and the Spokane, Portland and Seattle Railway on March 2, 1970 to form the Burlington Northern Railroad.

The Spokane, Portland & Seattle Railway was chartered in 1905 under the name of Portland & Seattle Railway by James J. Hill to connect his two transcontinental railroads (Northern Pacific and Great Northern) from Spokane, Washington, to Portland, Oregon. In January 1908, "Spokane" was added to the railroad's name making it the Spokane, Portland & Seattle Railway (SP&S). In 1910, the SP&S gained control of the Oregon Electric interurban railway which was extended south to Eugene by 1912. Hugging the north bank of the Columbia and Snake Rivers for 290 of the 380 miles between Portland and Spokane, the SP&S benefitted from those natural corridors with less motive power required to operate heavily lade freight trains and those river shores were natural settlements for a growing population. The Spokane, Portland & Seattle Railway was merged into the Burlington Northern Railroad on March 2, 1970.

The Burlington Northern Railroad (BNR) was created by the March 2, 1970 merger of the Great Northern Railway; Northern Pacific Railway; Spokane, Portland & Seattle Railway; and the Chicago, Burlington & Quincy Railroad. On November 21, 1980, the St. Louis–San Francisco Railway was acquired by BNR. Two independently operated railroads, owned by Burlington Northern Inc. were absorbed into the BNR; the Colorado & Southern Railway in 1981, and the Fort Worth & Denver Railway in 1982.

The Burlington Northern Santa Fe Railway resulted from the December 31, 1996 merger of the Atchison, Topeka & Santa Fe Railway with the Burlington Northern Railroad. On January 24, 2005, the name was shortened to BNSF Railway.

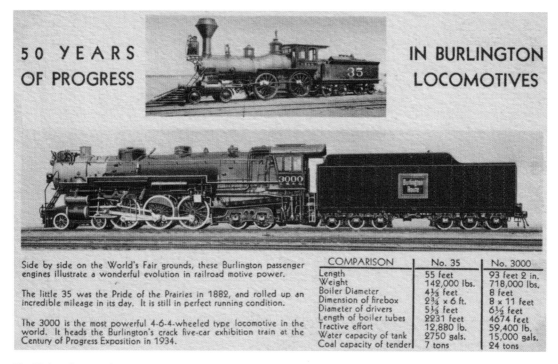

50 YEARS OF PROGRESS   IN BURLINGTON LOCOMOTIVES

Side by side on the World's Fair grounds, these Burlington passenger engines illustrate a wonderful evolution in railroad motive power.

The little 35 was the Pride of the Prairies in 1882, and rolled up an incredible mileage in its day. It is still in perfect running condition.

The 3000 is the most powerful 4-6-4-wheeled type locomotive in the world. It heads the Burlington's crack five-car exhibition train at the Century of Progress Exposition in 1934.

COMPARISON	No. 35	No. 3000
Length	55 feet	93 feet 2 in.
Weight	142,000 lbs.	718,000 lbs.
Boiler Diameter	4½ feet	8 feet
Dimension of firebox	2¾ x 6 ft.	8 x 11 feet
Diameter of drivers	5½ feet	6½ feet
Length of boiler tubes	2231 feet	4674 feet
Tractive effort	12,880 lb.	59,400 lb.
Water capacity of tank	2750 gals.	15,000 gals.
Coal capacity of tender	7 tons	24 tons

The 55-foot-long Burlington steam locomotive No. 35, *Pride of the Prairies*, was built in 1892 by the Chicago, Burlington & Quincy's Aurora, Illinois, Shops weighing 142,000 pounds, boiler diameter 4.5 feet, 5.5-foot diameter of drive wheels, tractive effort 12,880 pounds, water capacity of tank 2,750 gallons, and coal capacity of tender was 7 tons. It was on display at the 1934 Century of Progress World's Fair in Chicago alongside the 93.17-foot-long Burlington steam locomotive No. 3000. This class S-4 locomotive, with a 4-6-4 wheel arrangement, was built by Baldwin Locomotive Works in September 1930. It weighed 718,000 pounds, boiler diameter 8 feet, water capacity of tank 15,000 gallons, and coal capacity of tender was 24 tons. It was sold for scrap in April 1955. Side by side, these Burlington locomotives in this postcard scene showed the progress in railroad motive power. (*Kenneth C. Springirth collection*)

BURLINGTON ZEPHYR AT A CENTURY OF PROGRESS EXPOSITION — 1934
Built of stainless steel — Electric shot welded — Rides on articulated trucks. Powered by an eight-cylinder, two-cycle, 660 horse-power, oil-burning Diesel engine. Runs on roller-bearings — Air-conditioned—Equipped for radio reception.

The *Burlington Zephyr* is at the 1934 Century of Progress Exposition in this postcard scene. On May 26, 1934, this *Zephyr* ran 1,015 miles from Denver, Colorado, to Chicago in thirteen hours and five minutes, leaving Denver at 5:04 a.m. Mountain Time and arriving at Halsted Street in Chicago at 7:09 p.m. Central Time. Average speed was 77.6 miles per hour, and the top speed was 112.5 miles per hour. (*Kenneth C. Springirth collection*)

In 1958, Chicago, Burlington & Quincy Railroad steam locomotive No. 5090 (class 0-1-A built by Baldwin Locomotive Works in August 1918) is at the City of Savanna in Carroll County, Illinois. This Mikado type locomotive had a 2-8-2 wheel arrangement of two leading wheels on one axle usually in a leading truck, eight powered and coupled driving wheels on four axles, and two trailing wheels on one axle usually in a trailing truck. The name Mikado originated from Japanese 2-8-2 locomotives that were built in 1897 for the Nippon Railway of Japan. After the 1941 attack on Pearl Harbor, this type of locomotive was renamed MacArthur after General Douglas MacArthur. After the war, the locomotive was again known as a Mikado. (*Photographer Russ Porter Used with permission from Audio-Visual Designs [www.audiovisualdesigns.com]*)

Chicago, Burlington & Quincy Railroad (CB&Q) diesel rail motor No. 9841 is waiting for the next passenger trip between Galesburg and Peoria, Illinois, in the early 1960s. Built in July 1928 by EMD the car, also known as a "doodlebug," a short-line train, carried passengers plus mail and baggage. This was one of the few remaining rail motor cars on the CB&Q. It was scrapped in October 1961. (*Photographer D. Christensen-D.C. Wornom Collection Used with permission from Audio-Visual Designs [www.audiovisualdesigns.com]*)

CB&Q No. 9905 (named *Zephyrus*) with its shove nose design is the afternoon *Zephyr* making a stop at Winona, Wisconsin, in July 1950. This was one of the second pair of *Zephyrs* built in 1936. (*Photographer W.L. Heitter Used with permission from Audio-Visual Designs [www.audiovisualdesigns.com]*)

In April 1962, CB&Q type FT 1,350-horsepower diesel electric locomotive No. 113A (built in August 1944 by Electro Motive Corporation [EMC]) is at the Lincoln, county seat of Lancaster County, Nebraska, engine house waiting for the next assignment. The "F" stood for 1,400-horsepower (rounded from 1350) and "T" for twin as this locomotive was generally manufactured in semi-permanently coupled sets. (*Photographer Mac Owen Used with permission from Audio-Visual Designs [www.audiovisualdesigns.com]*)

On August 5, 1965, Burlington's Colorado & Southern Railway passenger train *Texas Zephyr* is ready to depart Colorado Springs, county seat of El Paso County, Colorado, for its southbound run to Dallas, Texas, powered by locomotive No. 9950A (built by EMD in March 1940) and Fort Worth & Denver B unit No. 9980. The October 28, 1962 schedule showed two passenger trains in each direction on this Denver via Amarillo and Fort Worth to Dallas route. (*Photographer Ed Fulcomer Used with permission from Audio-Visual Designs [www.audiovisualdesigns.com]*)

The April 1952 Official Guide of the Railways showed morning and afternoon Vista Dome Twin Zephyrs on their route between Chicago and Minneapolis.

A group of type E5 passenger diesel locomotives (headed by No. 9955 that was originally No. 9914A type E5A built by EMD in June 1941 for the Chicago Burlington & Quincy Railroad [CB&Q] and sold to the Colorado & Southern Railway [C&S] on September 20, 1961 becoming C&S No. 9955) are handling an extra freight movement on the Colorado & Southern Railway at Larkspur, a town in Douglas County, Colorado, in October 1967. After the C&S discontinued passenger service in 1967, the C&S E5's were place into freight service. These E5's, with their stainless steel bodies, were unique to the CB&Q. (*Burlington Route Used with permission from Audio-Visual Designs [www.audiovisualdesigns.com]*)

In the foreground is the Minnetonka, Northern Pacific Railway's first locomotive as it appeared in "Wheels A-Rolling," Chicago Railroad Fair pageant of transportation progress. The Minnetonka, built in 1870, is 27½ feet long, 10 feet 2 inches high, weighs 12 tons and costs $6,700. In comparison, the new 4500 H. P. Diesel locomotives which power the streamlined North Coast Limited are 151 feet 4 inches long, 15 feet high, weigh 345 tons and cost $458,000. The headend of one of the Diesels is shown in the background.

The Minnetonka, Northern Pacific Railway's first locomotive, is shown in the "Wheels A-Rolling" Chicago Railroad Fair pageant of transportation progress. This was one of four locomotives with a 0-4-0 wheel arrangement built in 1870 by Smith & Porter in Pittsburgh, Pennsylvania, in 1870. These locomotives were purchased to pull supply trains that were used to build the Northern Pacific Railway. The Minnetonka was 27.5 feet long, 10.17 feet high, weighed 12 tons, and cost $6,700. In comparison, the 4,500-horsepower diesel locomotive powering the North Coast Limited was 151.33 feet long, 15 feet high, weighed 345 tons, and cost $458,000. (*Kenneth C. Springirth collection*)

On June 24, 1941, Northern Pacific Railway steam locomotive No. 2456 is moving a box car at St. Paul, Minnesota. This locomotive was built by Alco in 1907 with a 2-6-2 wheel arrangement commonly known as a Prairie had two leading wheels, six coupled driving wheels, and two trailing wheels by Alco in 1907. (*Edward Wilde photograph*)

Northern Pacific Railway steam locomotive No. 1545 is powering a freight train at Minneapolis, Minnesota, on May 30, 1952. This Mikado-type locomotive, built by ALCO in 1905, had a 2-8-2 wheel arrangement with two leading wheels on one axle usually in a leading truck, eight powered and coupled driving wheels on four axles, and two trailing wheels on one axle usually in a trailing truck. (*Photographer Russ Porter Used with permission*)

On August 9, 1996, Northern Pacific Railway 1,750-horsepower EMD type F9A diesel electric locomotive No. 7010 is leading a set of four diesel units on a merchandise freight train at Logan, a community in Gallatin County, Montana. (*Photographer J.W. Swanberg Used with permission from Audio-Visual Designs [www.audiovisualdesigns.com]*)

On a winter snow-covered day, Great Northern Railway No. 201 (1,500-horsepower Alco diesel electric road switcher type RS-2 built in June 1947) is awaiting the next assignment at Vancouver, a city in Clark County, Washington. (*Mac Owen collection Used with permission from Audio-Visual Designs [www.audiovisualdesigns.com]*)

In June 1958, the Great Northern Railway's *Empire Builder* stops at the Chicago, Burlington & Quincy's Winona Junction Station on an eastbound run from Tacoma, Washington, and points west to Chicago, Illinois. A bus provided a connection to Winona, Minnesota. The Great Northern Railway (GNR) started the *Empire Builder* on June 10, 1929. After World War II, the GNR placed in service new streamlined and diesel-powered trains that cut the 2,211-mile trip between Chicago and Seattle from fifty-eight hours and thirty minutes to forty-five hours. (*Photographer Donald E. Smith Used with permission from Audio-Visual Designs [www.audiovisualdesigns.com]*)

Fairbanks Morse 1,000-horsepower type H-10-44 yard switcher No. 280 is ready for duty on the St. Louis–San Francisco Railway at Tulsa, a city and county seat of Tulsa County, Oklahoma. (*Photographer Mac Owen Used with permission from Audio-Visual Designs [www.audiovisualdesigns.com]*)

St. Louis–San Francisco Railway type M930 caboose No. 1776 is painted in the patriotic red, white, and blue paint scheme commemorating the United States Bicentennial. (*Photographer Mac Owen Used with permission from Audio-Visual Designs [www. audiovisualdesigns.com]*)

Four Santa Fe EMD SD45 diesel locomotives (each rated 3,600 horsepower) are powering a fast eastbound freight train near Kingman, the city and county seat of Mohave County, Arizona, in June 1967. (*Photographer Don Erb Used with permission from Audio-Visual Designs [www.audiovisualdesigns.com]*)

Fort Worth, Texas, in this 1973 postcard scene is the location of Santa Fe 1,750-horsepower diesel electric locomotive No. 287-C (EMD type F9 built in July 1956) in a yellow-on-blue paint scheme leading a group of locomotives in a variety of paint schemes.

An Atchison, Topeka & Santa Fe Railway (AT&SF) streamline passenger train powered at the head end by freight and passenger-hauling diesel locomotive No. 35 (1,500-horsepower EMD type F3 built in January 1949) is in Cajon Pass, a mountain pass between the San Bernardino Mountains to the east and the San Gabriel Mountains to the west in Southern California photographed in this postcard scene. With the summit of this pass 3,823 feet above sea level; completion of the line through the pass by the AT&SF was not easy. The final spike was driven on November 15, 1885, and the first train from San Diego used the route through the pass the next day. Amtrak's Southwest Chief uses this pass daily between Chicago and Loss Angeles on Burlington Northern Santa Fe Railway trackage.

On March 24, 1968, Santa Fe *Super Chief/El Capitan* is powered by two new 3,600-horsepower type FP45 diesel locomotives led by No. 108 that was built in December 1967 and was the last passenger locomotive ever purchased by the AT&SF. Geared for 95 miles per hour, this locomotive had a cowl body to provide sleeker looks, better aerodynamics at speed, and allowed the crew to enter the engine compartment *en route* for diagnostics and maintenance. (*Photographer Leo Caloia Used with permission from Audio-Visual Designs [www.audiovisualdesigns.com]*)

The eastbound Santa Fe *San Francisco Chief*, powered by a 2,000-horsepower Alco PA No. 60, built in 1948, and three PBs is passing through the countryside east of Belen in Valencia County, New Mexico, about 35 miles south of Albuquerque in August 1967. Alco's designation of "P" indicated the unit was geared for higher speeds and passenger train use. "A" indicated cab-equipped lead unit. "B" indicated cabless unit. (*Photographer Ken Crist Used with permission from Audio-Visual Designs [www.audiovisualdesigns.com]*)

Santa Fe locomotives Nos. 59 and 60 (type PA 2,000-horsepower diesel locomotive built by Alco in 1948) are shown at Colonie, a town in Albany County, New York, in December 1967. Both units were purchased by the Delaware & Hudson Railroad and later repainted in blue and yellow plus renumbered 16 and 17. They were used on the *Laurentian* and *Montreal Limited*. (*Photographer Jim Shaughnessy Used with permission from Audio-Visual Designs [www.audiovisualdesigns.com]*)

Santa Fe diesel locomotive No. 57 (type PA built by Alco in 1947) is at the Colorado Springs Station. As noted by the sign, the Denver & Rio Grande Western and Chicago, Rock Island & Pacific shared this station. (*Photographer Lewis A. Harlow Used with permission from Audio-Visual Designs [www.audiovisualdesigns.com]*)

Santa Fe Railway 3,600-horsepower diesel locomotive (in its blue and yellow freight colors) No. 1900, EMD type F45, built in June 1968, is leading a freight train near Williams, a city in Coconino County, Arizona, in October 1968. (*Santa Fe Railway photo Used with permission from Audio-Visual Designs [www.audiovisualdesigns.com]*)

A neat grouping of Santa Fe Railway freight and passenger diesels have been serviced and are positioned to handle freight and passenger assignments from the Argentine, Kansas, diesel shop that opened in the summer of 1954. (*Santa Fe Railway photo Used with permission from Audio-Visual Designs [www.audiovisualdesigns.com]*)

Santa Fe Railway four-axle 1,500-horsepower locomotive No. 2717 (EMD type GP7 built in 1952) looks sharp in the blue and yellow paint scheme in this September 1972 scene. (*Santa Fe Railway photo Used with permission from Audio-Visual Designs [www. audiovisualdesigns.com]*)

In September 1972, Santa Fe Railway 3,600-horsepower diesel electric locomotive No. 8712 (type U36C built by General Electric Company in 1972) sparkles in the September 1972 sunshine. (*Santa Fe Railway photo Used with permission from Audio-Visual Designs www.audiovisualdesigns.com]*)

On September 17, 1989, Santa Fe locomotive No. 101 (type FP45 built in December 1967) is on display at the Electro Motive Division of General Motors September 17, 1989 open house at La Grange, a village in Cook County, Illinois. (*Photographer John D. Bartley, Carl H. Sturner collection Used with permission from Audio-Visual Designs [www.audiovisualdesigns.com]*)

On September 15, 1990, a Santa Fe double-stack Maersk intermodal train is passing through the unincorporated community of Prewitt in McKinley County, New Mexico. Over the years, trailers and containers on flat cars have become increasingly popular as a way of moving goods over rail. (*Photographer Frank Ferguson Used with permission from Audio-Visual Designs [www. audiovisualdesigns.com]*)

1028

Burlington Lines

Burlington Route · **Everywhere West**

The Denver Zephyr—Overnight Every Night—No Extra Fare

CHICAGO, BURLINGTON & QUINCY RAILROAD COMPANY

Westbound—Read Down. | Table 1—CHICAGO, OMAHA, LINCOLN AND DENVER. | Eastbound—Read Up.

Vertical train designations (left to right):
To Kansas City and St. Joseph · American Royal · Zephyr 9902. Operates to Hannibal. See Table 9 · Motor. To Des Moines · Ak-Sar-Ben · Fast Mail. Coach passengers only · Denver Zephyr · California Zephyr, Chicago to San Francisco. See Note 1 on following page · Nebraska Zephyr · Coloradoan · Denver Zephyr · Coloradoan · Nebraska Zephyr · Ak-Sar-Ben · California Zephyr, San Francisco to Chicago. See Note 2 on following page · From Kansas City and St. Joseph · Zephyr 9902. Operates from Hannibal. See Table 9 · Motor. From Des Moines.

21	55	5	9	7	3	15	1	17	11	19	Mls.	January 27, 1952.	10	18	6	12	14	30	56	4	2	28
AM	PM	*PM	PM	AM	PM	PM	PM	PM	PM	AM		Central time.	AM	PM	PM	PM	AM	AM	AM	AM	AM	
*8 45	*6 30	a540	†3 15	*1215	*1000	*7 50	*5 00	*3 30	*1250	*1100	0	lv..+‖Chicago..ar.	9 05	1 30	9 30	8 45	7 00	8 10	8 25	11 20	11 35	
9 19	7 16	-	4 00	10 43	-	-	-	-	-	-	38	arr.+ Aurora..lve.	-	-	8 40	-	6 17	-	8 740	10 32	11055	
√9 33	7 20	-	4 10	1 11	10 45	-	-	□406	±1 07	-	38	lve..Aurora..arr.	n8 25	11 244	8 35	#7 57	6 10	7 17	8 733	10 27	11 054	
			4 20								40	...Montgomery...					5 58			10 15	f1 023	
		p6 27	4 27								46	.....Bristol......					5 49			10 06	11 034	
10 04		p6 32	4 34								52	+....Plano......			8 15		5 4i			9 54	11 027	
10 12			4 40								56	+..Sandwich.....					5 34			9 45		
10 17			4 48								59	+...Somonauk.....					5 24			9 35		
10 38			4 58								66	....Leland					5 15			9 25		
10 50											72	+...Earlville.....								9 17		
10 59											78	...Meriden.....								9 17		
11 09	8 04	a658	5 14	2 17	11 25				1 44		83	+..Mendota.....	7 45		5 02				a649	8 51	a1003	
			5 23								92	....Arlington								8 51		
			5 29								96	....Zearing								8 42		
			5 35								99	....Malden								8 35		
11 43	8 30	a717	5 45	2 43					2 03		104	+....Princeton	7 11						a622	8 28	a945	
			5 54								111	+....Wyanet	6 53							8 16		
	8 50		6 03								117	+....Buda								8 06		
			6 12								123	....Neponset								7 53		
1 08	9 15	a743	6 29	3 28	12 14				2 25		131	+..Kewanee	6 36	6 31						7 42	a923	
1 29	a927	a✶	6 55	3 50							139	+....Galva	6 21		4 02					7 28	a012	
			7 05								147	....Altona								7 14		
			7 22								151	....Oneida								7 08		
			7 29								155	....Wataga								7 01		
2 18	9 58	a816	7 40	4 20	12 45	10 20	7 07	5 45	2 55	a123	162	arr.+ Galesburg..lve.	6 48	10 58	5 50	6 00	3 35	5 15	*520	†6 50	a853	
	a818			4 45	1 00	10 35	7 09	5 50	3 00	a130	162	lve.‖ Galesburg..arr.	6 46	10 53	5 30	5 55	3 15	5 00			a851	
		a836		f4 58							172	....Cameron			5 16							
				5 12	fr 20					a154	179	+..Monmouth			5 06		2 45				a831	
				5 22							185	....Kirkwood			4 48							
				5 32							191*	....Biggsville			f4 35							
				5 42							196	....Gladstone ..			f4 28							
		a902		5 55	1 50	11 17	751	6 35	3 45	2 25	206	arr.+ Burlington..lve.	6 03	10 07	4 15	5 10	2 12	4 10			a805	
				6 40	1 50	11 32	751	6 35	3 45	2 25	206	lve.‖ Burlington..arr.	6 03	10 07	3 55	5 10	1 52	4 10			*AM	
				f6 55							210	...West Burlington..			f3 48							
				7 01							215	...Middletown....										
				7 11							219	....Danville			f3 38							
				7 29							225	...New London....			f3 31							
				f7 41		12 14			4 16		233	+.Mount Pleasant..			3 22		1 24					
				8 03							240	....Rome			3 07							
				8 18		12 50					244	...Lockridge			3 03							
									4 37		255	+..Fairfield			2 54	4 21	1 259					
			27								266	+...Batavia			2 36							
			AM								274	...Agency City ..			f2 29							
			8 37	306	1 24	856		7 46	5 03	3 35	280	arr.+ Ottumwa .. lve.	4 53	8 55	2 20	3 55	12 59					
			9 15	3 10	1 39	858		7 48	5 05	3 40	280	lve.‖ Ottumwa .. arr.	4 51	8 53	2 10	3 53	12 15	2 47				
			9 29								288	...Chillicothe			f1 59						10 55	
										409	....Avery									f1037	
			9 50		2 24						304	+...Albia		1 40			1145				†10 24	
			10 10								319	...Melrose									†10 15	
			10 22								327	...Russell									PM	
			10 42		3 10					446	335	+..Chariton		1 01		2 57	11 05					
			10 54								343	...Lucas										
			11 05								351*	...Woodburn										
			11 24		3 48					5 20	360	+..Osceola		1227			10 25					
			11 38								371*	+...Murray					10 11					
			f11 43								376	...Thayer										
91			11 55								384	....Afton					9 55					
AM			1207	5 10	4 25	1042		9 42	6 56	5 53	393	arr.+‖Creston..lve.	3 07	7 02	11 50	2 05	9 40	12 42				
†7 30			12 22	5 20	4 35	1044		9 45	6 59	5 59	393	lve..Creston..arr.	3 05	6 58	11 45	2 03	9 30	12 35				
7 45											399	...Cromwell					9 18					
8 00			●1237		5 03						407	+...Prescott			11 19		9 07					
8 40			12 46						±6 19		414	+...Corning					8 57					
8 50											418	....Brooks					8 46					
9 01											423	...Nodaway					8 40					
9 35			1 08		5 25					6 38	428	+..Villisca			11 03		8 33					
9 55			1 18								435	...Stanton					8 19					
10 30			1 37	√6 14	5 55			■1030	-	7 03	443	+..‖Red Oak			10 42	1 18	8 08	⟩				
AM			1 53								452	...Emerson					7 41					
Mixed.			2 03								457	...Hastings, Ia....					7 31					
			2 12								462	+..Malvern					7 25					
			2 30								472	+..Glenwood					7 16					
			f2 36								475	arr...Pacific Jn...lve.					7 10					
											480	+..Plattsmouth ..										
			2 59	♯7 15			Ψ1208		f8 00		492	arr.+‖Council Bluffs..lv.			1229		10 46					
			3 25	7 45	7 30	1 12				8 20	493	arr.‖Council Bluffs Trans..lv.										
			3 40	8 00	7 45	12 30	11 45	9 00	8 35		496	+....Omaha	*1 15	*5 00	*9 25	*1215	*6 30	*1030				
			PM	AM	AM	AM	PM	PM	PM			ARRIVE] [LEAVE	AM	AM	AM	PM	PM	PM				

🚌 Rail-Auto Service available at this point.

Continued on following page.

*Daily; †daily, except Sunday; a does not carry checked baggage to or from this station; f stops to let off revenue passengers or on signal to receive revenue passengers; n stops to let off revenue passengers from Denver; p stops to let off revenue passengers—does not carry checked baggage to or from this station; r stops to receive revenue passengers for Chicago when notified at Mendota—does not carry checked baggage to or from this station; s stops Sunday; t stops to leave revenue passengers from west of Denver; y commutation tickets not honored; z stops to receive revenue passengers. √ Tickets reading via the C. B. & Q. from Chicago to Galesburg and intermediate stations will be honored west of Aurora on American Buslines bus No. 7-7B. □ Stops to receive revenue passengers for Omaha or beyond. ● Stops to let off revenue passengers from Osceola and east or to receive for Omaha or beyond. Ψ Stops to let off revenue passengers from Chicago. ♯ Stops to let off revenue passengers. ■ Stops to discharge revenue passengers from Chicago or receive revenue passengers for Denver when notified at Creston.

(Right margin) Stops daily to discharge revenue passengers from Chicago and on Sunday only to receive revenue passengers or on signal to receive revenue passengers for Chicago. ⊡ Stops to receive revenue passengers from Chicago. ♯ Stops to let off revenue sleeping car passengers from Chicago.

For Equipment of these trains, see pages 1022-1027.

Stops daily to discharge revenue passengers from Chicago and on Sunday only to receive revenue passengers for Omaha or beyond when notified by 2:00 p.m. ‖ Meal stop. + Coupon stations.

The Burlington Lines January 27, 1952 schedule shows passenger service from Chicago, Illinois, via Aurora, Illinois, to Omaha, Nebraska, from the *April 1952 Official Guide of the Railways.*

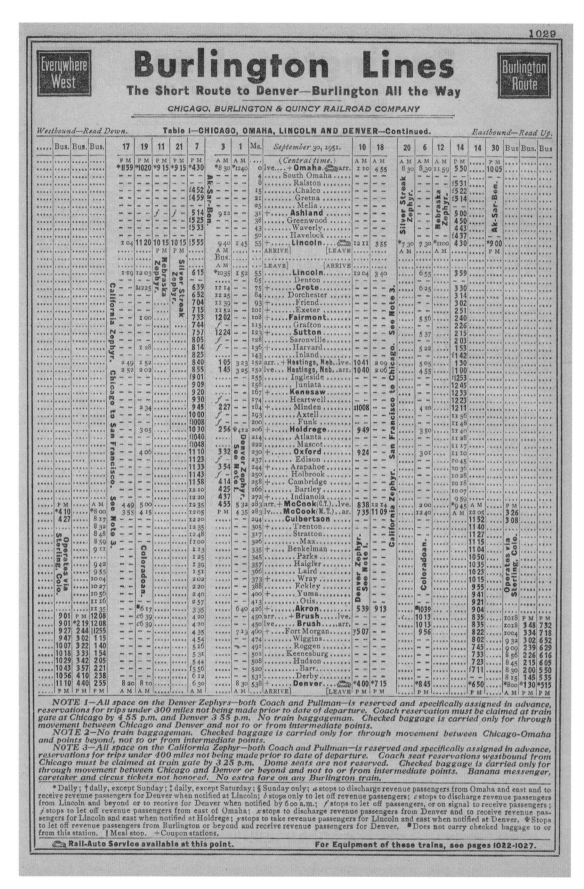

This is a continuation of the Burlington Lines schedule from Omaha, Nebraska, to Denver, Colorado, from the *April 1952 Official Guide of the Railways*.

947

Automatic Block Signals or Train Control

Santa Fe

Santa Fe

COAST-TO-COAST SLEEPING CAR SERVICE

New York, Washington, Chicago, Kansas City and California, via The Santa Fe Chief

Through Sleepers between New York and Los Angeles, via New York Central 20th Century Limited and Pennsylvania Railroad Broadway Limited East of Chicago—thence, via the Santa Fe Chief ... Through Sleeper between Washington and San Diego, via Baltimore & Ohio Capitol Limited to Chicago, thence the Santa Fe Chief.

TABLE B — WESTBOUND.

DAILY.	20th Cent.Ltd N.Y.C. Sys.	B'way Ltd. Penna. R.R.	Capitol Ltd. B.&O. R.R.	
Lve. New York (E.T.)	6 00 P M	6 00 P M		
Lve. North Philadelphia		7 21 P M		
Lve. Washington			5 30 P M	
Lve. Pittsburgh (E.T.)		1 52 A M	12 10 A M	
Arr. Chicago (C.T.)	9 00 A M	9 00 A M	8 00 A M	

Mls	STATIONS. See Rules on page 948.	No. 19—THE CHIEF. Extra Fare.	
		Daily	By Days
0	Lve. Chicago (C.T.) (A.T.&S.F.)	1 30 P M	Sun Mon Tue Wed Thu Fri Sat
451	Arr. Kansas City	9 50 P M	Sun Mon Tue Wed Thu Fri Sat
....	Lve. St. Louis	(Mo. Pac.) 4 00 P M	(Wabash) 4 00 P M
....	Arr. Kansas City	9 00 P M	9 00 P M
451	Lve. Kansas City (A.T.&S.F.)	10 15 P M	Sun Mon Tue Wed Thu Fri Sat
563	Lve. Emporia	12 15 A M	Mon Tue Wed Thu Fri Sat Sun
636	Lve. Newton (C.T.)	1 45 A M	Mon Tue Wed Thu Fri Sat Sun
789	Lve. Dodge City (M.T.)	3 20 A M	Mon Tue Wed Thu Fri Sat Sun
992	Arr. La Junta	6 25 A M	Mon Tue Wed Thu Fri Sat Sun
1271	Lve. Lamy	1 00 P M	Mon Tue Wed Thu Fri Sat Sun
1338	Lve. Albuquerque	2 30 P M	Mon Tue Wed Thu Fri Sat Sun
1490	Lve. Gallup	5 05 P M	Mon Tue Wed Thu Fri Sat Sun
1627	Lve. Winslow	7 10 P M	Mon Tue Wed Thu Fri Sat Sun
1719	Lve. Williams	9 15 P M	Mon Tue Wed Thu Fri Sat Sun
1742	Arr. Ash Fork	10 05 P M	Mon Tue Wed Thu Fri Sat Sun
1770	Lve. Seligman (M.T.)	11 10 P M	Mon Tue Wed Thu Fri Sat Sun
1919	Arr. Needles (P.T.)	1 00 A M	Tue Wed Thu Fri Sat Sun Mon
1919	Lve. Needles	1 10 A M	Tue Wed Thu Fri Sat Sun Mon
2086	Arr. Barstow	4 15 A M	Tue Wed Thu Fri Sat Sun Mon
2164	Arr. San Bernardino	6 30 A M	Tue Wed Thu Fri Sat Sun Mon
2215	Arr. Pasadena (See Note‡)	7 55 A M	Tue Wed Thu Fri Sat Sun Mon
2224	Arr. Los Angeles	8 30 A M	Tue Wed Thu Fri Sat Sun Mon

CONNECTING TRAINS

0	Lve. Ash Fork (A.T.&S.F.)	2 00 A M	Tue Wed Thu Fri Sat Sun Mon
194	Arr. Phoenix	8 30 A M	Tue Wed Thu Fri Sat Sun Mon
0	Lve. Barstow (A.T.&S.F.)	♮6 20 A M	Tue Wed Thu Fri Sat Sun Mon
461	Arr. San Francisco	♮5 25 P M	Tue Wed Thu Fri Sat Sun Mon
0	Lve. Pasadena {Motor}	8 20 A M	Tue Wed Thu Fri Sat Sun Mon
35	Arr. Long Beach {Coach}	9 35 A M	Tue Wed Thu Fri Sat Sun Mon
0	Lve. Los Angeles (A.T.&S.F.)	11 30 A M	Tue Wed Thu Fri Sat Sun Mon
128	Arr. San Diego	2 15 P M	Tue Wed Thu Fri Sat Sun Mon

EASTBOUND.

Mls	STATIONS. See Rules on page 948.	No. 20—THE CHIEF. Extra Fare.	
		Daily	By Days
0	Lve. Los Angeles (P.T.) (A.T.&S.F.)	12 30 P M	Sun Mon Tue Wed Thu Fri Sat
9	Lve. Pasadena (See Note‡)	1 00 P M	Sun Mon Tue Wed Thu Fri Sat
60	Lve. San Bernardino	2 18 P M	Sun Mon Tue Wed Thu Fri Sat
138	Lve. Barstow	4 30 P M	Sun Mon Tue Wed Thu Fri Sat
305	Arr. Needles	7 13 P M	Sun Mon Tue Wed Thu Fri Sat
305	Lve. Needles (P.T.)	7 23 P M	Sun Mon Tue Wed Thu Fri Sat
454	Arr. Seligman (M.T.)	11 30 P M	Sun Mon Tue Wed Thu Fri Sat
482	Arr. Ash Fork	12 15 A M	Mon Tue Wed Thu Fri Sat Sun
505	Lve. Williams	1 29 A M	Mon Tue Wed Thu Fri Sat Sun
597	Lve. Winslow	3 42 A M	Mon Tue Wed Thu Fri Sat Sun
725	Lve. Gallup	5 42 A M	Mon Tue Wed Thu Fri Sat Sun
886	Lve. Albuquerque	8 30 A M	Mon Tue Wed Thu Fri Sat Sun
953	Lve. Lamy	9 40 A M	Mon Tue Wed Thu Fri Sat Sun
1232	Lve. La Junta (M.T.)	4 10 P M	Mon Tue Wed Thu Fri Sat Sun
1435	Lve. Dodge City (C.T.)	8 20 P M	Mon Tue Wed Thu Fri Sat Sun
1588	Arr. Newton	10 45 P M	Mon Tue Wed Thu Fri Sat Sun
1773	Arr. Kansas City	1 50 A M	Tue Wed Thu Fri Sat Sun Mon
....	Lve. Kansas City	(Mo. Pac.) 7 01 A M	(Wabash) 7 00 A M
....	Arr. St. Louis	12 01 P M	11 59 A M
1773	Lve. Kansas City (A.T.&S.F.)	2 05 A M	Tue Wed Thu Fri Sat Sun Mon
2224	Arr. Chicago (C.T.)	10 30 A M	Tue Wed Thu Fri Sat Sun Mon

DAILY.	20th Cent.Ltd N.Y.C. Sys.	B'way Ltd. Penna. R.R.	Capitol Ltd. B.&O. R.R.	
Lve. Chicago (C.T.)	4 30 P M	4 30 P M	4 30 P M	
Arr. Pittsburgh (E.T.)		1 24 A M	2 01 A M	
Arr. Washington			8 55 A M	
Arr. North Philadelphia		8 01 A M		
Arr. New York (E.T.)	9 30 A M	9 30 A M		

CONNECTING TRAINS

0	Lve. San Diego (A.T.&S.F.)	7 45 A M	Sun Mon Tue Wed Thu Fri Sat
128	Arr. Los Angeles	10 30 A M	Sun Mon Tue Wed Thu Fri Sat
0	Lve. Long Beach {Motor}	11 25 A M	Sun Mon Tue Wed Thu Fri Sat
35	Arr. Pasadena {Coach}	12 30 P M	Sun Mon Tue Wed Thu Fri Sat
0	Lve. Phoenix (A.T.&S.F.)	5 00 P M	Sun Mon Tue Wed Thu Fri Sat
194	Arr. Ash Fork	11 15 P M	Sun Mon Tue Wed Thu Fri Sat

♮ Via train No. 23 Barstow to Bakersfield, then train No. 61 Bakersfield to San Francisco—No. 23 arrives Bakersfield 10 50 a.m., No. 61 leaves Bakersfield 11 20 a.m. ■ Stops to receive paying passengers for New Mexico, Arizona or California points where scheduled to stop, see note page 948. **Note ‡**—Gateway to Hollywood, Beverly Hills, Glendale and Santa Monica.

EQUIPMENT—Lightweight Streamlined Standard Sleeping Cars only.

No. 19—Daily (The Chief). Completely Air-Conditioned.

Valet, Barber Service, Men's and Women's Shower Bath and Radio. Extra Fare from Chicago and Kansas City $10.00. (Federal Tax not included.)

Baggage Lounge Car..Chicago to Los Angeles.
Sleeping Cars..Chicago to Los Angeles—17 Roomettes.
 New York to Los Angeles—2 D.R., 4 Compts., 4 Double Bedrooms and 10 Roomettes, 6 Double Bedrooms. (Via N. Y. C. Train 25 to Chicago.)
 New York to Los Angeles—2 Drawing-rooms, 4 Compts., 4 Double Bedrooms. (Via P. R. R. Train 29 to Chicago.)
 Washington to San Diego—13 Roomettes, 6 Double Bedrooms. (Via B. & O. Train 5 to Chicago.)
 Chicago to Phoenix—2 Drawing-rooms, 4 Compartments, 4 Double Bedrooms (on No. 47 from Ash Fork).
Club Lounge Car..Chicago to Los Angeles.
Dining Car.....Chicago to Los Angeles. (Cafe-Parlor Car Ash Fork to Phoenix.) (Fred Harvey Service.)

Sleeping Car...Chicago to Los Angeles—2 D.R., 4 Compts., 4 D.B.R.
Observation Car..Chicago to Los Angeles—4 D.R., 1 Double Bedroom.
Santa Fe Parlor-Lounge Car..Los Angeles to San Diego (on connecting train).

No. 20—Daily (The Chief). Completely Air-Conditioned.

Valet, Barber Service, Men's and Women's Shower Bath and Radio. Extra Fare to Kansas City and Chicago $10.00. (Federal Tax not included.)

Baggage Lounge Car..Los Angeles to Chicago.
Sleeping Cars..Los Angeles to Chicago—17 Roomettes.
 Los Angeles to New York—2 D.R., 4 Compts., 4 Double Bedrooms and 10 Roomettes, 6 Double Bedrooms. (Via N. Y. C. Train 26 from Chicago.)
 Los Angeles to New York—2 Drawing-rooms, 4 Compts., 4 Double Bedrooms. (Via Pennsylvania R.R. Train 28 from Chicago.)
 San Diego to Washington — 10 Roomettes, 6 Double Bedrooms. (Via B. & O. train No. 6 from Chicago.)
 Phoenix to Chicago—2 Drawing-rooms, 4 Compartments, 4 Double Bedrooms (on No. 42 to Ash Fork).
Club Lounge Car..Los Angeles to Chicago.
Dining Car ....Los Angeles to Chicago. (Cafe-Parlor Car Phoenix to Ash Fork.) (Fred Harvey Service.)

Sleeping Car...Los Angeles to Chicago—2 D.R., 4 Compts., 4 D. B.R.
Observation Car..Los Angeles to Chicago—4 D.R., 1 Double Bedroom.
Santa Fe Parlor-Lounge Car..San Diego to Los Angeles (on connecting train).

The Santa Fe Coast to Coast sleeping car service is shown from New York City via Chicago, Illinois, and Kansas City to Los Angeles, California, from the *April 1952 Official Guide of the Railways*.

Santa Fe passenger service from Chicago via Amarillo and Belen to Los Angeles, California, along with passenger service from Los Angeles to San Diego, and from Barstow via Los Angeles to San Francisco is shown from the *April 1952 Official Guide of the Railways*.

691

ST. LOUIS-SAN FRANCISCO RAILWAY CO.
SERVING THE
SOUTHEAST AND SOUTHWEST

Table 1—ST. LOUIS, TULSA AND OKLAHOMA CITY.

March 2, 1952.

5	3	9	1	Mls.	LEAVE ARRIVE	4	10	2	6
PM	PM	PM	PM			AM	AM	AM	PM
*215	*1120	*700	*530	0	+....St. Louis....🚗	725	745	810	415
225	1130	710	540	3.3	+..Tower Grove....	705	725	750	357
x—	— —	— —	— —	10.1	...Webster Groves....	c650	g710	e737	c344
x242	— —	— —	— —	12.7	....Kirkwood......	— —	— —	— —	f —
f —	— —	— —	— —	24.9	....Crescent......	— —	— —	— —	f —
309	— —	— —	— —	34.1	....Pacific.......	— —	— —	— —	309
f —	— —	— —	— —	39.0	...Catawissa......	— —	— —	— —	f —
f320	— —	— —	— —	40.8	...Robertsville....	— —	— —	f258	f —
f330	— —	— —	— —	46.2	....Moselle......	— —	— —	f250	f —
344	— —	— —	— —	52.3	....St. Clair.....	— —	— —	241	— —
f —	— —	— —	— —	57.3	...Anaconda......	— —	— —	— —	— —
f359	— —	— —	— —	62.3	....Stanton......	— —	— —	f229	— —
410	— —	— —	— —	68.1	...Sullivan......	— —	— —	222	— —
f420	— —	— —	— —	74.4	....Bourbon......	— —	— —	f209	— —
f —	— —	— —	— —	79.6	...Leasburg......	— —	— —	f —	— —
436	— —	— —	— —	86.9	....Cuba.......	512	— —	151	— —
f —	— —	— —	— —	91.4	....Fanning......	— —	— —	— —	— —
f453	— —	— —	— —	94.9	....Rosati......	— —	— —	f138	— —
504	— —	— —	— —	100.5	...St. James.....	x448	— —	130	— —
f511	— —	— —	— —	105.7	....Dillon......	— —	— —	f122	— —
530	■140	■925	b742	110.7	+....Rolla......	435	■510	e547	115
545	155	940	757	119.2	arr. +Newburg..lve.	415	455	532	1255
◈	◈	◈	◈		....Fort Leonard Wood	◈	◈	◈	◈
605	205	945	801	119.2	lve...Newburg...arr.	405	450	528	1230
— —	— —	— —	— —	123.2	...Arlington.....	— —	— —	— —	■1220
— —	— —	— —	— —	124.0	....Jerome......	— —	— —	— —	— —
f620	— —	— —	— —	129.0	....Franks......	— —	— —	— —	f12 11
630	— —	— —	— —	134.7	....Dixon......	— —	— —	— —	1202
f —	— —	— —	— —	140.1	...Hancock......	— —	— —	— —	f —
651	— —	— —	— —	146.7	....Crocker.....	— —	— —	— —	11 41
f700	— —	— —	— —	152.3	...Swedeborg.....	— —	— —	— —	f1129
713	— —	— —	— —	159.9	...Richland.....	— —	— —	— —	11 16
728	— —	— —	— —	167.6	...Stoutland....	— —	— —	— —	11 03
f736	— —	— —	— —	174.3	....Sleeper.....	— —	— —	— —	f1052
758	■325	■107	b921	181.9	+...Lebanon.....	230	■325	e413	1041
— —	— —	— —	— —	187.5	..Brush Creek....	— —	— —	— —	— —
f815	— —	— —	— —	194.0	..Phillipsburg...	— —	— —	— —	f1020
f824	— —	— —	— —	198.5	....Conway......	— —	— —	— —	f1013
f835	— —	— —	— —	207.0	...Niangua.....	— —	— —	— —	f1002
845	— —	— —	— —	213.5	+..Marshfield....	— —	— —	— —	f9 52
f854	— —	— —	— —	220.1	..Northview....	— —	— —	— —	f9 42
f905	— —	— —	— —	228.0	...Strafford....	— —	— —	— —	f9 33
930	450	1225	1025	239.3	ar.+Springfield..lv.	115	210	310	*9 15
PM	515	1245	1040	239.3	lve..Springfield.arr.	1240	200	255	AM
	— —	— —	— —	248.2	...Brookline....	— —	— —	— —	
	— —	— —	— —	252.8	...Republic....	— —	— —	— —	
	— —	— —	— —	258.3	...Billings....	— —	— —	— —	
	— —	— —	— —	263.3	....Logan.....	— —	— —	— —	
	— —	— —	— —	264.6	..Marionville...	— —	— —	— —	
	600	b120	b11 15	269.9	+...Aurora.....	1201	f120	e220	
	— —	— —	— —	274.6	....Verona....	— —	— —	— —	
	625	140	f1135	283.0	arr.+Monett..lve.	1130	100	0205	
	640	200	f1135	283.0	lve....Monett...arr.	1100	1245	0205	
	— —	— —	— —	287.9	+..Pierce City...	— —	— —	— —	
	— —	— —	— —	298.2	...Ritchey....	— —	— —	— —	
	— —	— —	— —	302.9	....Granby....	— —	— —	— —	
	725	■238	— —	310.8	+...Neosho....	1025	■1203	— —	
					(Camp Crowder.)				
	— —	— —	— —	320.2	....Racine....	— —	— —	— —	
	r746	— —	— —	326.3	...Seneca....	■948	— —	— —	
	— —	— —	— —	334.1	..Wyandotte...	— —	— —	— —	
	— —	— —	— —	341.6	...Fairland...	— —	— —	— —	
	812	h331	— —	349.1	+....Afton....	921	■11 14	— —	
	835	352	— —	360.7	+...Vinita....	905	■1100	— —	
	r859	— —	AM	380.2	+...Chelsea....	e835	*—		
	918	442	— —	398.7	+..Claremore...	815	■1017	*—	
	1000	530	— —	424.6	arr.+Tulsa🚗lve.	740	945	AM	
	1020	— —	— —	424.6	lve....Tulsa...arr.	720	925		
	f1031	— —	— —	431.7	...Oakhurst...	f702	— —		
	f1033	— —	— —	433.6	...Bowden....	f700	— —		
	1038	h618	— —	438.5	+..Sapulpa...	654	■903		
	f1055	— —	— —	446.8	...Kellyville..	f638	— —		
	11 16	h645	— —	460.2	+...Bristow...	617	— —		
	f1127	— —	— —	467.7	+...Depew....	601	■835		
	f1133	— —	— —	473.5	....Milfay....	f553	— —		
	f1144	— —	— —	478.7	...Stroud....	546	— —		
	f1155	— —	— —	486.4	..Davenport...	533	— —		
	1211	h727	— —	495.1	+..Chandler...	518	■752		
	f1226	— —	— —	504.0	...Warwick...	f502	— —		
	f1230	— —	— —	506.7	..Wellston...	f457	— —		
	f1244	— —	— —	515.9	....Luther....	f445	— —		
	f1258	— —	— —	524.4	....Jones....	f432	— —		
	f1 07	— —	— —	531.9	...Spencer...	f421	— —		
	130	825	— —	541.8	+..Oklahoma City🚗	*405	*700		
	PM	AM			ARRIVE LEAVE	PM	PM		

For additional trains between Tulsa and Sapulpa, see Table 16, page 695.

Table 2.
ROLLA AND FORT LEONARD WOOD—Bus service by Frisco Transportation Co.

Bus.	Bus.	Bus.	Bus.	*February*, 1952.	Bus.	Bus.	Bus.	Bus.	Bus.
*940 PM	*540 PM	*100 PM	*600 AM	lve.........Rolla.........arr.	1240 PM	110 PM	650 PM	815 PM	110 AM
1000 PM	600 PM	120 PM	620 AM	lve........Newburg.....lve.	1220 PM	— —	630 PM	755 PM	1250 AM
1100 PM	650 PM	210 PM	710 AM	arr.Fort Leonard Wood..lve.	*1120 AM	k1215 PM	*530 PM	*655 PM	*1150 PM

For number of table upon which each station is located, see General Index of Stations in back part of Guide.

EXPLANATION OF SIGNS.

* Daily.

† Daily, except Sunday.

§ Sunday only.

b Stops to receive revenue passengers for Oklahoma and Texas.

c Stops to discharge revenue passengers.

e Stops to discharge revenue passengers from Oklahoma and Texas.

f Stops on signal to take on or let off passengers.

g Stops to discharge revenue passengers from Springfield or beyond.

h Stops on signal to discharge revenue passengers from St. Louis and beyond and to receive revenue passengers for Oklahoma City and beyond.

i Stops to discharge revenue passengers from St. Louis and beyond and to receive revenue passengers for Oklahoma and Texas.

k Saturday only.

o Stops to discharge revenue passengers from Texas and Oklahoma and on signal to receive revenue passengers for St. Louis or beyond.

r Stops to let off revenue passengers from Springfield or beyond and stop on signal to take on revenue passengers for Tulsa and beyond.

t Stops on signal to receive revenue Pullman passengers for St. Louis and beyond.

x Stops to receive revenue passengers.

z Stops to let off revenue passengers from Springfield or beyond and stop on signal to receive revenue passengers for St. Louis.

♮ Stops to let off revenue passengers from St. Louis and beyond and on signal to take on revenue passengers for Ft. Smith and Oklahoma City or beyond.

■ Stops on signal to take on or let off revenue passengers.

◈ Fort Leonard Wood is reached by bus service of the Frisco Transportation Company between Rolla-Newburg, Mo., and Fort Leonard Wood. See bus schedules Table 2.

● Stops to let off revenue passengers from Tulsa and beyond and on signal to take on revenue passengers for Springfield and beyond.

+ Coupon stations.

STANDARD— *Central time.*

🚗 Rail-Auto Service available at this point.

1095

ROUTE OF THE *Streamlined* NORTH COAST LIMITED

Table I—MAIN LINE TRAINS.

111	123	1-13	11	141	No. 3	No. 1	Mls	February, 1952.	No. 2	No. 4	12	14-2	112	124	STOP-OVERS.
		PM	AM		(Diesel-Powered.)			(Central time.)		(Diesel-Powered.)	PM	AM			Stop-overs on one-way tickets allowed at any point en route within thirty (30) days from date of sale.
		*1100	*845		*100 PM	*1100 PM		...Chicago (C.B.& Q.)...	745 AM	240 PM	240	745			
		800	300		745 PM	800 AM		arr.St. Paul » lve.	1045 PM	825 AM	825	1045			*Daily.
		AM	PM					(Central time.)			AM	PM			†Daily, except Sunday.
	*900	*815			*930 PM	*900 AM	0	lve. + St. Paul ®Ⓣ☖...arr.	1000 PM	730 AM	715	1000			
	925	840			955 »	925 »	11	arr.+ Minneapolis ®Ⓣ☖lv.	935 »	705 »	650	935			d Stops only to leave passengers from west of Little Falls.
	935	855			1015 »	935 »	11	lve.+ Minneapolis...arr.	927 »	655 »	640	927			
		926			— —	— —	29	+......Anoka........		d621 »	558	— —			f Stops on flag.
					— —	— —	36	+.......Dayton.......				— —			x Stops to discharge revenue passengers from Fargo and east and pickup revenue passengers for Billings and west for points where train No. 1 is scheduled to stop.
	1016	939			— —	1016 »	40	+.......Elk River......	842 »	d605 »	fs35	842			
		f949			— —	— —	49	+......Big Lake.......		d553 »	519	— —			
		f957			— —	— —	57	+.....Becker........		d544 »	504	— —			
		f1004			— —	— —	64	+.....Clear Lake......		d535 »	451	— —			
	1052	1021			1137 PM	1052 »	76	+.......St. CloudⓉ.....	804 »	519 »	430	804			
		1023			— —	— —	77	+.....Sauk Rapids.....		d504 »	424	— —			
		f1026			— —	— —	80	+.......Sartell.......		d501 »	418	— —			
		f1036			— —	— —	90	+........Rice........		d452 »	357	— —			y Stops for revenue passengers only.
		f1042			— —	— —	97	+......Royalton......		d446 »	345	— —			
	1125	1105			1220 AM	1125 AM	107	+.....Little FallsⓉ....	729 »	431 »	*325	729			z Stops to discharge revenue passengers from Billings and west and to pick up revenue passengers for Fargo and east for points where train No. 2 is scheduled to stop.
		PM			f1238 »		118	+......Randall......		410 »	AM				
					f1246 »		123	+......Cushing......		402 »					
					f1255 »		129	+......Lincoln......		352 »					
					f104 »		135	+......Philbrook.....		342 »					
	1201				115 AM	1201 PM	141	arr.......StaplesⓉ....lve.	647 PM	330 AM		647			△ Stops to receive and discharge passengers only.
	AM										PM				
	*735				*740 PM	*735 AM	141	lve. + DuluthⓉ,☖...arr.	1050 PM	810 AM		1050			‖ Meals.
	750				752 PM	750 AM		lve.+SuperiorⓉ...arr.	1034 »	754 »		1034			® Station Restaurant.
AM	1145				1240 AM	1145 AM		arr.......StaplesⓉ....lve.	650 PM	330 AM		650	PM		
†600	1211				135 AM	1211 PM	141	lve.+......Staples......arr.	640 PM	320 AM		640	555		Ⓣ Pullman tickets sold at this station.
610	— —				— —	— —	148	+......Aldrich......		f307 »			541		
620	— —				f152 »	— —	152	+......Verndale.....		f300 »			535		+ Coupon stations.
630	1234				206 »	1234 »	159	+......WadenaⓉ.....	616 »	248 »		616	†523		
AM					214 »	— —	164	+......Bluffton.....		233 »			PM		
	— —				228 »	— —	172	+...New York Mills...		217 »					*Mountain Standard time* is used by the Northern Pacific Railway Company between Mandan and North Dakota-Montana State Line. *Central Standard time* (which is one hour in advance of Mountain Standard time) is the time adopted for use by the State of North Dakota between the same points.
	101				248 »	101 »	182	+......Perham Ⓣ....	547 »	201 »		547			
					308 »	— —	193	+......Frazee......		142 »					
	125				329 »	125 »	203	+...Detroit LakesⓉ..	522 »	124 »		522			
					345 »	— —	210	+......Audubon.....		108 »					
					402 »	— —	216	+.....Lake Park.....		1257 »					
	PM				413 »	— —	222	+.......Dale......		AM			PM		
*504	155				— —	155 »	224	+..Manitoba Junction..	450 »	*450 »			136		
510	PM				423 »	— —	228	+......Hawley......		1236 »			124		
†520					— —	— —	234	+......Muskoda.....		PM			f115		
532					451 »	— —	242	+......Glyndon.....		1210 AM			102		
542	137				510 »	— —	247	+......Dilworth.....		1158 PM			AM		
550	Mix.				516 »	f240 »	251	+.......MoorheadⓉ...	f410 »	1145 »		138	1253		z Stops to discharge revenue passengers from Billings and west and to pick up...
555					530 »	245 »	252	arr.......+ FargoⒷⓉ....lve.	407 »	1140 »		Mix.	1244		
PM					550 »	255 »	252	lve.......Fargo........arr.	400 »	1115 »		PM	*1240		
		733			600 »	— —	257	+.....West Fargo.....		1100 »		530	PM		
		750			609 »	— —	264	+.....Mapleton.....		f1049 »		516			
		810			620 »	— —	272	+.....CasseltonⓉ....		1036 »		455			
		AM			632 »	— —	278	+......Wheatland....		1023 »		†440			
					649 »	— —	288	+......Buffalo......		1003 »		PM			
					659 »	— —	294	+.....Tower City....		955 »					
					709 »	— —	299	+......Oriska......		942 »					
			AM		730 »	407 »	310	arr.+ Valley CityⓉ..lve.	248 »	920 »	142				
			†800		745 »	407 »	310	lve.+ Valley City....arr.	248 »	911 »	PM				
					— —	— —	314	+.......Berea.....		AM	210				
			825		f804 »	— —	320	+......Sanborn.....		f853 »		†145			
			AM		f812 »	— —	326	+......Eckelson....		844 »		PM			
					f824 »	— —	333	+......Spiritwood...		831 »					
					843 »	459 »	344	arr.+ JamestownⒷⓉ..lve.	205 »	810 »					
					905 »	504 »	344	lve.......Jamestown....arr.	200 »	745 »					
					920 »	— —	351	+......Eldridge....		730 »					
					932 »	— —	360	+......Windsor.....		718 »					
					939 »	— —	364	+......Cleveland....		710 »					
					950 »	— —	373	+......Medina......		655 »					
					1001 »	— —	381	+...Crystal Springs...		641 »					
					1012 »	— —	389	+......Tappen.....		628 »					
					1025 »	x557 »	394	+......Dawson......	z104 »	616 »					
	176				1036 »	606 »	402	+.......Steele.....	1254 »	606 »		175			
	Mix.				1052 »	— —	413	+......Driscoll....		538 »		Mix.			
	PM				1103 »	— —	421	+......Sterling....		526 »		AM			
	†400				1116 »	— —	427	+.....McKenzie Ⓣ...		512 »		1050			
	408				f1125 »	— —	433	+......Burleigh....		f502 »		1032			
	515			AM	1158 AM	710 »	440	+.....BismarckⓉ,☖..	1210 PM	445 »		1005			
	535			AM	1240 PM	730 »	451	arr.+ Mandan (C.T.)ⒷⓉ.lve.	1150 AM	420 »		†935			
	PM				101 »	740 »	451	lve.+ Mandan (C.T.)...arr.	1140 »	355 »		AM			
					1201 »	640 »	451	lve.+ Mandan (M.T.)...arr.	1040 »	255 »					
							467	+.....Sweet Briar....		220 »					
					1232 »	— —	473	+......Judson......		210 »					STANDARDS—East of Mandan, *Central time*; between Mandan and Paradise, *Mountain time*; west of Paradise, *Pacific time*.
					1242 »	— —	479	+.....New Salem....		210 »					
					1251 »	— —	484	+....North Almont...		201 »					
					117 »	746 »	500	+......Glen Ullin....	†939 »	136 »					
					136 »	— —	512	+......Hebron......		115 »					
					f150 »	— —	521	+......Antelope....		f103 »					
					159 »	— —	527	+.....Richardson...		1254 »					
					207 »	— —	532	+.......Taylor.....		1245 »					
					219 »	— —	540	+......Gladstone....		1234 »					
					f228 »	— —	547	+.......Lehigh.....		f1224 »					
					236 PM	857 PM	552	arr.+ DickinsonⓉ..lve.	*835 AM	*1216 PM					
								(Mountain time.)							

Main Line continued on following page.

The Northern Pacific Railway schedule passenger service is shown from Chicago to Dickinson from the *April 1952 Official Guide of the Railways.*

NORTHERN PACIFIC RAILWAY
"Main Street of the Northwest"

1096

Table 2—MAIN LINE TRAINS—Continued.

Bus.	Bus.	No. 221	No. 3	No. 1	Mls	March, 1952.	No. 2	No. 4	No. 222	Bus.	Bus.
						LEAVE (Mountain time.) ARRIVE					
			*2 44 PM	*9 02 PM	552	+.........Dickinson Ⓣ.........	8 30 AM	12 07 PM			
			2 59 "	– –	562	..........South Heart..........	– –	11 49 AM			
			3 14 "		572	+............Belfield............		11 35 "			
			3 24 "		578	.............Fryburg..............		11 25 "			
			f3 32 "		583	..........Sully Springs..........		f11 16 "			
			3 44 "		591	+.............Medora.............		11 03 "			
					603	..............Demores............		– –			
			4 07 "		608	+.........Sentinel Butte.........		10 38 "			
			4 21 "	10 32 "	616	+...Beach, North Dakota.....	7 05 "	10 25 "			
			4 36 "	– –	627	+..............Wibaux............	– –	10 08 "			
			f4 52 "		637	...............Hodges...........		f9 49 "			
			5 23 "	11 30 "	657	arr........+Glendive ®Ⓣ...lve.	6 10 "	9 20 "			
			5 43 "	11 40 PM	657	lve...........Glendive......arr.	6 00 "	1 05 "			
			6 10 "	– –	677	...............Marsh.............	– –	12 35 "			
			6 24 "		687	................Fallon............		f12 19 "			
			6 36 "	f12 31 AM	697	+................Terry...........	o5 11 "	12 03 AM			
			#6 55 "		710	................Benz.............		f11 37 PM			
			7 33 "	1 27 "	736	+...........Miles City Ⓣ.........	4 18 "	10 57 "			
			f8 07 "	– –	756	...............Hathaway..........	– –	f10 24 "			
			8 26 "		760	...............Rosebud..........		10 05 "			
			8 48 "	2 35 "	781	arr........+Forsyth ®Ⓣ...lve.	3 15 "	9 45 "			
			8 53 "	2 40 "	781	lve...........Forsyth......arr.	3 10 "	9 35 "			
			a9 21 "	– –	802	+...............Sanders.........	– –	a8 57 "			
			9 31 "		809	+...............Hysham.........		8 47 "			
			a9 38 "		814	...............Myers............		a8 38 "			
			a9 53 "		824	+..............Big Horn.........		a8 23 "			
			10 01 "		830	................Custer...........		8 15 "			
			a10 31 "		852	...........Pompey's Pillar.......		a7 41 "			
			a10 45 "		862	...............Worden..........		f7 26 "			
			f10 56 "		870	...............Huntley..........		7 13 "			
			11 15 PM	4 55 AM	883	arr.......+Billings ®Ⓣ.🚗.lve.	*1 00 AM	*6 55 PM			
				#11 15 AM		arr.....Cody (C.B. & Q.)....lve.	*7 45 PM	x105 PM			
						(Yellowstone Park.)					
			*7 45 PM			lve.....Cody (C.B. & Q.)....arr.	#11 15 AM				
			*11 40 PM	*5 10 AM	883	lve.......+Billings ®.🚗.arr.	12 50 AM	*6 35 PM			
					895	..............Mossmain..........		– –			
			12 04 AM		808	+...............Laurel Ⓣ.........		6 08 "			
			12 18 "		906	..............Park City..........		5 55 "			
			12 45 "	f6 03 "	923	+..............Columbus Ⓣ.......	f11 59 PM	5 30 "			
			1 12 "		940	+.............Reed Point........		5 06 "			
			f1 29 "		953	..............Greycliff..........		4 46 "			
			1 46 "	6 57 "	964	+.............Big Timber Ⓣ.......	11 14 "	4 31 "			
			fa 09 "		979	..............Springdale........		4 08 "			
			2 45 AM	7 45 AM	999	+.............Livingston Ⓣ.......	*10 35 PM	*3 40 PM			
						ARRIVE LEAVE					
			#10 15/10 15	10 15/10 15	1053	+..............Gardiner Ⓣ........	#7 30 PM	#11 30 AM			
						(Yellowstone Park.)					
			#7 30 PM	#7 30 PM		lve.........+Gardiner......arr.	10 15/2 10 15				
						LEAVE ARRIVE					
			*3 00 AM	*8 00 AM	999	+..............Livingston........	10 25 PM	3 30 PM			
			4 02 "	8 58 "	1023	+.............Bozeman Ⓣ.🚗......	9 30 "	2 35 "			
			4 18 "	– –	1033	+...............Belgrade........	– –	2 11 "			
			4 35 "		1042	...............Manhattan........		1 59 "			
			4 50 AM	9 30 AM	1047	arr.........+Logan ®.......lve.	*8 50 PM	*1 50 PM			
		*9 40 AM	*5 00 AM		1047	+..............Logan ®..........	1 35 PM	8 25 PM			
		9 49 "	f5 09 "		1053	+...............Trident.........	f1 26 "	f8 11 "			
		10 10 "	f5 32 "		1068	+..............Lombard.........	1 03 "	7 47 "			
		10 26 "	5 47 "		1077	................Toston..........	f12 43 "	7 29 "			
		10 44 "	6 09 "		1088	+..............Townsend........	12 26 PM	7 14 "			
		11 03 "			1100	..............Winston..........	– –	6 55 "			
					1110	..............Louisville.........					
		11 26 "			1121	+............East Helena........		6 38 "			
AM		11 35 AM	7 10 AM		1121	arr..........+Helena ®Ⓣ.🚗.lve.	*11 43 AM	*6 30 PM	PM		
*11 15			*7 30 AM		1121	lve..........Helena.🚗....arr.	11 15 AM		6 25		
			f7 59 "		1134	................Austin..........	f10 46 "				
12 20			f8 28 "		1142	...............Blossburg........	10 25 "				
f–			8 42 "		1150	...............Elliston..........	10 04 "		5 35		
			8 56 "		1159	................Avon............	9 48 "		f–		
1 05			f9 06 "		1165	...............Bradley..........	fg 38 "				
PM			9 20 AM		1172	+..............Garrison ®........	*9 20 AM		*5 05		
						ARRIVE LEAVE					
				No. 1				No. 2			
AM		*5 20 AM	*9 35 AM		1047	+..............Logan ®..........	8 40 PM	1 25	PM		
		5 35 "	– –		1054	+..............Three Forks.......	– –	1 10			
		5 45 "			1060	+.............Willow Creek.......		1 00			
					1079	...............Cardwell.........		– –			
		6 30 "	10 40 AM		1086	+...............Whitehall........	7 47 "	12 20			
		– –			1108	...............Homestake.🚗....	– –				
		7 30 AM	12 15 PM		1118	+..............Butte ®Ⓣ (M.T.).🚗..	*6 30 PM	*11 00	AM		
						ARRIVE LEAVE					

Main Line continued on following page.

For number of table upon which each station is located, see General Index of Stations in back part of Guide.

EXPLANATION OF SIGNS.

* Daily.
† Daily, except Sunday.
§ Sunday only.
a Stops to pick up or let off passengers to and from Forsyth and east and Billings and west.
f Stops on flag.
o Stops to discharge passengers from Spokane and beyond or to take passengers for Minneapolis, St. Paul or beyond.
? Stops to leave passengers from St. Paul or Minneapolis and beyond and to take passengers for Spokane and beyond.
x Daily, via bus.
Stops on flag for revenue passengers only.
■ Daily, June 18 to September 8.
Ψ Connection daily, except Sun., via bus approximately September 9 to June 17, 1952.
Ɛ Daily bus service available only during Park season, June 18 to September 8.
‖ Meals.
® Station Restaurant.
Ⓣ Pullman tickets sold at this station.
+ Coupon stations.
🚗 Rail-Auto Service available at this point.

Mountain Standard time is used by the Northern Pacific Railway Company between Mandan and North Dakota - Montana State Line.

Central Standard time (which is one hour in advance of Mountain Standard time) is the time adopted for use by the State of North Dakota between the same points.

The Northern Pacific Railway schedule passenger service is shown from Dickinson to Butte from the *April 1952 Official Guide of the Railways.*

1097

ROUTE OF THE *Streamlined* NORTH COAST LIMITED

Table 3—MAIN LINE TRAINS—Continued.

Bus.	Bus.	No. 5	287		No. 3	No. 1	Mls	February 26, 1952.	No. 2	No. 4		288	Bus.	Bus.
		A M						LEAVE] (Mount. time.) [ARRIVE		A M				
		*7 45				*12 25 P M	1118	+......Butte ℗⊤......	6 20 P M	11 00				
		f7 55				- -	1125	......Silver Bow......	- -	10 43				
		f8 07				- -	1133	......Durant......	- -	f10 28				
		f8 12				- -	1137	......Stuart......	- -	f10 22				
		8 21				- -	1144	+......Warm Springs......	- -	10 11				
		8 41		RUNS VIA HELENA.	1 19 »	11 59 »	1170	+......Deer Lodge⊤......	5 21 P M	9 48				
		9 00			1 35 P M	1170 arr.	+......Garrison ℗......lve.	5 05 P M	*9 30	See connecting service to Butte in adjoining column.			
		A M			*9 30 A M	*1 40 P M	1170 lve.	......Garrison......arr.	5 00 P M	9 05 A M		A M		
					f9 42 »	- -	1178	......Gold Creek......	- -	8 54 »		11 00		
					10 05 »	y2 05 »	1190	+......Drummond......	z4 36 »	8 34 »		10 43		
					f10 19 »	- -	1200	......Bearmouth......	- -	f8 14 »		f10 28		
				Connects with No. 3.	f10 50 »	- -	1222	......Clinton......	- -	7 45 »		f10 22		
					11 05 »	- -	1232	......Bonner......	- -	7 31 »		10 11		
P M	A M				11 15 »	3 00 »	1238 arr.	+......Missoula ℗⊤......lve.	3 45 »	7 20 »		9 48		
†3 15	†5 30				11 35 A M	3 15 »	1238 lve.	......Missoula ℗⊤......arr.	3 35 »	7 00 »		*9 30	P M	P M
						- -	1245	......De Smet......	- -	f -			1 05	3 00
P M	A M				n12 14 P M	- -	1256	......Evaro......	- -	c6 19 »			f -	f -
4 00	f -				12 36 »	- -	1266	+......Arlee......	*2 32 »	5 46 »				
4 20	7 00				1 00 »	- -	1276	+......Ravalli......	- -	5 29 »			†12 05	1 45
P M	8 00				1 12 »	- -	1283	+......Dixon......	- -	f5 17 »			P M	†1 25
	A M				1 30 »	- -	1297	......Perma......	- -	4 59 »				P M
					2 10 »	5 10 »	1304 arr.	+...Paradise ℗ (Mount. time) lve.	1 35 »	4 40 »				
					1 20 »	4 15 »	1309 lve.	...Paradise (Pacific time)...arr.	12 30 P M	3 35 »				
					1 33 »	- -	1315	+......Plains......	- -	3 21 »				
					2 13 »	4 55 »	1341	+......Thompson Falls......	11 48 A M	2 34 »				
					f2 42 »	- -	1363	......Trout Creek......	- -	f1 48 »				
					f2 50 »	- -	1369	......Tuscor......	- -	f1 36 »				
					3 03 »	- -	1379	+......Noxon......	- -	1 18 »				
					3 17 »	- -	1389	......Heron, Mont......	- -	1 00 »				
						- -	1400	......Colby, Idaho......	- -	- -				
					3 32 »	- -	1403	+......Clark's Fork......	- -	f12 36 »				
					3 45 »	- -	1413	+......Hope......	- -	12 20 A M				
					4 13 »	6 39 »	1428	+......Sandpoint⊤......	10 12 »	11 53 P M				
					f4 41 »	- -	1449	+......Granite......	- -	f11 10 »				
					4 53 P M	*7 16 P M	1456 arr.	+......Athol......lve.	n9 35 A M	10 59 P M				
								......lve.......Farragut......arr.						
					4 53 P M	*7 16 P M	1456 lve.	......Athol⊤......arr.	n9 35 A M	10 59 P M				
					5 13 »	- -	1469	+......Rathdrum......	- -	10 40 »				
					f5 22 »	- -	1476	......Hauser, Idaho......	- -	f10 27 »				
				Diesel-Powered.	6 00 P M	8 10 »	1496 arr.	+......Spokane ℗⊤......lve.	8 50 »	9 45 »	North Coast Limited—Diesel-Powered.			
						8 40 »	1496 lve.	......Spokane......arr.	8 25 »	7 30 »				
		*7 15 A M					1505	......Marshall......	- -	- -				
		7 41 »				f9 05 »	1512	+......Cheney⊤......	f7 57 »	7 01 »				
		8 15 »				f9 33 »	1537	+......Sprague⊤......	7 25 »	6 26 »				
		8 44 »				10 01 »	1561	+......Ritzville⊤......	f6 58 »	5 56 »				
		9 05 »				10 18 »	1578	+......Lind......	z6 39 »	5 30 »				
		9 47 »				f10 53 »	1606	+......Connell......	6 03 »	4 50 »				
		10 30 A M				11 40 P M	1642 arr.	+......Pasco ℗⊤......lve.	5 25 A M	4 05 P M				
		*10 40 A M				*1 35 A M	1642 lve.	......Pasco......(S. P. & S.) arr.	2 30 A M	3 45 P M				
		4 35 P M				7 00 A M	1874 arr.	...Portland ℗ (Un. Sta)......lve.	*9 15 P M	*9 00 A M				
		10 45 A M				11 59 P M	1642 lve.	......Pasco......arr.	5 15 A M	3 50 P M				
		10 57 »				12 11 A M	1644	+......Kennewick⊤......	4 59 »	3 40 »				
		f11 28 A M				- -	1665	......Kiona......	- -	f3 13 »				
		12 02 P M				1 03 »	1681	+......Prosser⊤......	4 11 »	2 53 »				
		12 19 »				f1 18 »	1693	+......Mabton......	f3 57 »	2 37 »				
						- -	1707	......Alfalfa......	- -	- -				
		12 46 »				1 44 »	1712	+......Toppenish⊤......	3 37 »	2 14 »				
		1 00 P M				1 57 A M	1719	+......Wapato⊤......	3 24 A M	2 02 P M				
							1675	......Gibbon......						
			Runs via Prosser and Toppenish				1695	......Sunnyside......	Runs via Toppenish and Prosser	Runs via Toppenish and Prosser				
							1710	......Zillah......						
							1722	......Parker......						
		1 30 P M				2 20 A M	1731 arr.	+......Yakima⊤......lve.	1 45 P M					
		1 35 »				2 30 »	1731 lve.	......Yakima⊤......arr.	3 00 »	1 35 »				
		1 40 »				- -	1735	+......Selah......	- -	1 23 »				
		2 37 »				3 33 »	1768	+......Ellensburg⊤......	2 00 »	12 25 »				
		f2 50 »				- -	1775	+......Thorp......	- -	f12 07 P M				
		3 18 »				4 12 »	1792	+......Cle Elum⊤......	1 15 »	11 37 A M				
		3 36 »				4 29 »	1805	+......Easton......	12 57 »	11 19 »				
		4 29 »				5 21 »	1827	+......Lester......	12 04 A M	10 24 »				
		f5 01 »				- -	1841	+......Eagle Gorge......	- -	f9 47 »				
		5 17 »				- -	1850	+......Kanaskat......	- -	9 30 »				
		f5 27 »				- -	1855	......Ravensdale......	- -	f9 18 »				
		5 50 P M				6 35 A M	1869 arr.	+......East Auburn......lve.	10 45 A M	8 55 A M				
		6 01 P M				6 46 A M	1869 lve.	......East Auburn......arr.	10 17 A M	8 34 A M				
		6 07 »				6 53 »	1870	+......Auburn⊤......lve.	10 13 »	8 30 »				
		6 08 »				6 54 »	1874 lve.	+......Auburn......arr.	10 13 »	8 30 »				
		6 19 »				7 05 »	1878	+......Sumner⊤......	9 59 »	8 13 »				
		6 26 »				7 12 »	1881	+......Puyallup⊤......	9 54 »	8 06 »				
		6 45 P M				7 30 A M	1889 arr.	+......Tacoma ℗⊤......lve.	*9 40 P M	*7 50 A M				
		6 00 P M				6 45 A M	1869 lve.	......East Auburn......arr.	10 35 A M	8 45 A M				
		6 03 »				- -	1870	......Auburn⊤......lve.	- -	8 40 »				
		6 05 »				- -	1870 lve.	+......Auburn......arr.	- -	8 40 »				
		6 15 »				k6 58 »	1875	+......Kent⊤......	f8 30 »					
		6 45 P M				7 30 A M	1892 arr.	+......Seattle ℗⊤......lve.	*1000 P M	*8 05 A M				
								(Pacific time.)						

Notes (right column):

*Daily; †daily, except Sunday.

a Stops to discharge passengers from east of Missoula—on Sunday stops on flag.

c Stops on flag Sunday only.

f Stops on flag.

g Stops to leave passengers from Walla Walla, Spokane and east.

i Stops on flag to discharge passengers from Missoula and east or to receive for Pasco and west where scheduled to stop.

n Stops on flag to discharge passengers from Pasco and west or to receive for Missoula and east where scheduled to stop.

y Stops to leave passengers from east of Fargo and to pick up passengers for Spokane and west.

z Stops on flag to leave passengers from Spokane and west and to pick up passengers for east of Fargo.

♭ Stops to pick up or leave passengers to and from stations east of Spokane and west of Pasco where scheduled to stop.

■ Stops on flag—passengers destined to Ronan and Polson should detrain at Arlee in order to make connection with Northern Pacific Transport bus; detail of this schedule in Table 32.

℗ Station Restaurant.

⊤ Pullman tickets sold at this station.

‖ Meals.

+ Coupon stations.

(left margin): For number of table upon which each station is located, see General Index of Stations in back part of Guide.

(left margin): Rail-Auto Service available at this point.

The Northern Pacific Railway schedule passenger service is shown from Butte to Seattle from the *April 1952 Official Guide of the Railways.*

PAGE 6

CONDENSED SCHEDULES—PASSENGER TRAINS

Streamlined EMPIRE BUILDER
Detailed Schedules Begin on Page 10, Table 1

West—Read Down   East—Read Up

Example by days	Empire Builder 31 Daily	Central Standard Time — Burlington Route	Empire Builder 32 Daily	Example by days
...... Mon	2 00	Lv Chicago...Table 1.Ar	2 00	Wed ....
...... Mon	8 40	Ar St. Paul.............Lv	7 15	Wed ....
		Great Northern Railway		
...... Mon	9 10	Lv St. Paul....Table 1.Ar	7 00	Wed ....
...... Mon	9 35	Ar Minneapolis.Table 1.Lv	6 30	Wed ....
...... Mon	9 40	Lv Minneapolis.........Ar	6 25	Wed ....
...... Mon	11 12	Lv Willmar.............Lv	4 40	Wed ....
...... Tue	12 55	" Breckenridge........"	2 42	Wed ....
...... Tue	1 45	Ar Fargo................Lv	1 30	Wed ....
...... Tue	1 50	Lv Fargo................Lv	1 23	Wed ....
...... Tue	3 49	" New Rockford Tbl. 4 "	11 07	Tue ....
...... Tue	5 26	Ar Minot...............Lv	9 12	Tue ....
...... Tue	5 35	Lv Minot................Ar	9 02	Tue ....
...... Tue	7 55	Ar Williston...Table 4 .Lv	6 50	Tue ....
		Mountain Standard Time		
...... Tue	7 05	Lv Williston...........Ar	5 40	Tue ....
...... Tue	▲ 8 56	" Wolf Point...........Lv	▲ 3 40	Tue ....
...... Tue	▲ 9 45	" Glasgow.............Lv	▲ 2 45	Tue ....
...... Tue	12 15	Ar Havre....Table 6 .Lv	12 01	Tue ....
...... Tue	12 25	Lv Havre...............Ar	11 50	Tue ....
...... Tue	▲ 1 28	Lv Chester.............Lv	▲10 46	Tue ....
...... Tue	2 15	" Shelby....Table 6 ."	10 03	Tue ....
...... Tue	▲ 2 48	" Cut Bank..........."	▲ 9 35	Tue ....
...... Tue	5 55	Ar Whitefish............Lv	6 30	Tue ....
...... Tue	6 00	Lv Whitefish............Lv	6 25	Tue ....
...... Tue	8 50	Ar Troy.................Lv	3 30	Tue ....
		Pacific Standard Time		
...... Tue	7 50	Lv Troy......Table 9.Ar	2 30	Tue ....
...... Tue	11 20	Ar Spokane.............Lv	11 05	Mon ....
...... Tue	11 50	Lv Spokane.............Ar	10 35	Mon ....
...... Wed	2 14	" Ephrata.............Lv	8 18	Mon ....
...... Wed	3 20	Ar Wenatchee.Table 10 Lv	7 20	Mon ....
...... Wed	3 35	Lv Wenatchee..........Ar	7 17	Mon ....
...... Wed	6 45	Ar Everett..............Lv	4 18	Mon ....
...... Wed	6 55	Lv Everett..............Ar	4 18	Mon ....
...... Wed	■ 7 16	" Edmonds............Lv	♦ 3 58	Mon ....
...... Wed	7 50	Ar Seattle Tbl 10-11-12 Lv	3 30	Mon ....
...... Wed	9 12	Ar Tacoma...Table 12 .Lv	12 05	Mon ....

	1 Daily	Spokane, Portland & Seattle Ry.	2 Daily	
...... Tue	11 59	Lv Spokane............Ar	10 25	Mon ....
...... Wed	2 45	Ar Pasco...............Lv	7 25	Mon ....
...... Wed	5 00	Ar Wishram............Lv	5 05	Mon ....
...... Wed	6 50	Ar Vancouver, Wash...Lv	3 23	Mon ....
...... Wed	7 15	Ar Portland Tables 12-13 Lv	3 00	Mon ....

▲Conditional stop. See Tables 6 and 8.
■Westbound Empire Builder and Western Star will stop to discharge revenue passengers.
♦Eastbound Empire Builder and Western Star will stop to receive revenue passengers.

For connections to and from California see Table 15.

Streamlined WESTERN STAR
Detailed Schedules Begin on Page 11, Table 2

West—Read Down   East—Read Up

Example by days	Western Star 3 Daily	Central Standard Time — Burlington Route	Western Star 4 Daily	Example by days
...... Mon	11 10	Lv Chicago...Table 2.Ar	7 55	Thur ....
...... Tue	7 30	Ar St. Paul.............Lv	11 45	Wed ....
		Great Northern Railway		
...... Tue	8 30	Lv St. Paul....Table 2.Ar	10 10	Wed ....
...... Tue	8 55	Ar Minneapolis Table 2 .Lv	9 45	Wed ....
...... Tue	9 00	Lv Minneapolis.........Ar	9 35	Wed ....
...... Tue	10 20	" St. Cloud.........."	8 15	Wed ....
...... Tue	11 12	" Sauk Centre........"	7 18	Wed ....
...... Tue	11 37	" Alexandria.........."	6 47	Wed ....
...... Tue	12 31	" Fergus Falls........"	5 48	Wed ....
...... Tue	1 07	" Barnesville........."	5 09	Wed ....
...... Tue	1 36	" Moorhead..........."	4 38	Wed ....
...... Tue	1 39	Ar Fargo...............Lv	4 35	Wed ....
...... Tue	1 49	Lv Fargo...............Ar	4 23	Wed ....
...... Tue	3 14	Ar Grand Forks Table 2.Lv	2 52	Wed ....
...... Tue	3 25	Lv Grand Forks........Ar	2 40	Wed ....
...... Tue	5 25	Lv Devils Lake........"	12 58	Wed ....
...... Tue	7 55	Ar Minot...............Lv	10 30	Wed ....
...... Tue	8 05	Lv Minot................Ar	10 20	Wed ....
...... Tue	10 30	Ar Williston...Table 5 .Lv	7 50	Wed ....
		Mountain Standard Time		
...... Tue	9 50	Lv Williston...........Ar	6 40	Wed ....
...... Wed	12 50	" Glasgow.............Ar	3 45	Wed ....
...... Wed	3 50	Ar Havre....Table 6 .Lv	12 45	Wed ....
...... Wed	4 10	Lv Havre...............Ar	12 30	Wed ....
...... Wed	7 15	Ar Great Falls.........Lv	9 30	Tue ....
...... Wed	7 40	Lv Great Falls.........Ar	9 10	Tue ....
...... Wed	10 20	" Shelby....Table 7 .Lv	6 30	Tue ....
...... Wed	10 55	Lv Cut Bank..........."	5 55	Tue ....
...... Wed	12 20	" Glacier Park●......"	4 55	Tue ....
...... Wed	2 10	" Belton●............"	2 55	Tue ....
...... Wed	2 30	" Columbia Falls......"	2 30	Tue ....
...... Wed	2 50	" Whitefish..........."	2 15	Tue ....
...... Wed	5 40	Ar Troy......Table 9 .Lv	11 15	Tue ....
		Pacific Standard Time		
...... Wed	4 50	Lv Troy......Table 9.Ar	10 10	Tue ....
...... Wed	8 15	Ar Spokane.............Ar	7 10	Tue ....
...... Wed	9 00	Lv Spokane.............Ar	6 30	Tue ....
...... Wed	11 15	Lv Ephrata.............Lv	4 10	Tue ....
...... Thur	12 23	Ar Wenatchee.Table 10 Lv	2 45	Tue ....
...... Thur	12 35	Lv Wenatchee..........Ar	2 30	Tue ....
...... Thur	f 2 53	Lv Skykomish..Table 10 Lv	f12 20	Tue ....
...... Thur	4 11	Ar Everett..............Lv	11 10	Mon ....
...... Thur	4 30	Lv Everett..............Ar	10 49	Mon ....
...... Thur	■ 4 54	" Edmonds............Lv	♦10 30	Mon ....
...... Thur	* 5 30	Ar Seattle.Tbl 10-11-12 Lv	10 00	Mon ....
...... Thur	9 12	Ar Tacoma....Table 12 Lv	8 33	Mon ....

	3 Daily	Spokane, Portland & Seattle Railway	4 Daily	
...... Wed	9 45	Lv Spokane............Ar	6 10	Tue ....
...... Thur	5 30	Ar Vancouver, Wash...Lv	10 10	Mon ....
...... Thur	6 00	Ar Portland Tables 12-13 Lv	9 45	Mon ....

*Sleeping cars and coaches may be occupied until 7:30 A. M.
f—Flag stop for revenue passengers.

●The Western Star stops at Glacier Park and Belton, eastern and western rail entrances to Glacier National Park, June 15 thru September 10.

Time from 12.01 midnight to 12.00 noon shown in light face type; time from 12.01 noon to 12.00 midnight shown in heavy face type.

The June 9, 1957 Great Northern Railway condensed schedule is shown for the Empire Builder and Western Star. (*Beth Anne Keates collection*)

Page **4**

Condensed Schedules of Main Line Trains

EMPIRE BUILDER—WESTERN STAR
CHICAGO-TWIN CITIES-SPOKANE-SEATTLE-TACOMA-PORTLAND

WESTBOUND—Read Down   EASTBOUND—Read Up

27 Western Star Daily (1 day for example)	31 Great Dome Empire Builder Daily (1 day for example)	Miles	Table A — Empire Builder features — Recorded Music, Radio, Coach Porter Service	32 Great Dome Empire Builder Daily (1 day for example)	28 Western Star Daily (1 day for example)
	12 30 Su	0	Lv **Chicago, Ill.** (C.T.) ...... Ar	3 15 We	
	1 10 Su	38	" **Aurora, Ill.** .... Ar	2 24 We	
	3 30 Su	186	" **E. Dubuque, Ill.** .... Ar	11 57 We	
	5 08 Su	297	" **La Crosse, Wis.** .... Ar	10 23 We	
	5 46 Su	326	" **Winona Jct., Wis.**	9 45 We	
	7 45 Su	427	Ar **St. Paul** Lv	8 15 We	
8 30 Mo	8 25 Su	427	Lv **St. Paul** .... Ar	7 20 We	6 15 We
9 05 Mo	8 55 Su	437	" **Minneapolis, Minn.** ... Ar	6 30 We	5 40 We
1 50 Mo	1 47 Mo	689	" **Fargo, N. Dak.** .... Ar	12 25 We	12 45 We
3 20 Mo		768	Lv **Grand Forks** Lv		11 15 We
7 50 Mo	5 25 Mo	922	" **Minot**	8 55 Tu	7 00 Mo
9 20 Mo	6 40 Mo	1042	" **Williston, N. Dak. (M.T.)** Ar	5 20 Tu	3 10 Mo
3 00 Tu	11 50 Mo	1351	" **Havre, Mont.** Lv	12 20 Tu	8 20 Tu
6 10 Tu	3 00 Mo	1474	Ar **Great Falls** ①③ Lv	8 30 Tu	5 00 Tu
f 6 34 Tu	c 3 15 Mo	1527	Lv **Glacier Park** Lv	c 8 40 Tu	f 4 20 Tu
f 8 16 Tu	c 4 55 Mo	1584	" **Belton, Mont.** .... "	c 6 50 Tu	f 2 40 Tu
2 30 Tu	10 50 Mo	1881	" **Spokane, Wash. (P.T.)** .. "	11 40 Mo	7 00 Tu
9 14 Tu	6 05 Tu	2178	Ar **Everett** .... "	4 45 Mo	11 10 Mo
10 30 Tu	7 30 Tu	2211	Ar **Seattle** Lv	3 45 Mo	10 00 Mo
8 57 We	8 57 Tu		Ar **Tacoma, Wash.** Lv	1 38 Mo	7 53 Mo
5 30 We	7 00 Tu	2260	Ar **Portland, Ore.** Lv	3 00 Mo	9 45 Mo

c—Conditional stop. The Empire Builder stops at Glacier Park and Belton, eastern and western rail entrances to Glacier National Park, during the summer season.

NORTH COAST LIMITED—MAINSTREETER
CHICAGO-TWIN CITIES-SPOKANE-SEATTLE-TACOMA-PORTLAND

WESTBOUND—Read Down   EASTBOUND—Read Up

29 The Mainstreeter Daily (1 day for example)	25 Vista-Dome North Coast Limited Daily (1 day for example)	Miles	Table B — North Coast Limited features — Recorded Music, Radio, Stewardess Service, Coach Porter Service	26 Vista-Dome North Coast Limited Daily (1 day for example)	30-10 The Mainstreeter Daily (1 day for example)
	12 30 Su	0	Lv **Chicago, Ill.** (C.T.) ...... Ar	3 15 We	11 15 Th
	1 10 Su	38	" **Aurora, Ill.** .... "	2 24 We	10 30 Th
	3 30 Su	186	" **E. Dubuque, Ill.** .... "	11 57 We	8 11 Th
	5 08 Su	297	" **La Crosse, Wis.** .... Ar	10 23 We	6 26 We
	5 46 Su	326	" **Winona Jct., Wis.** ...... "	9 45 We	5 52 We
	7 45 Su	427	Ar **St. Paul** Lv	8 15 We	4 30 We
7 30 Mo	8 15 Su	427	Lv **St. Paul** .... Ar	7 50 We	2 55 We
8 05 Mo	8 43 Su	437	" **Minneapolis, Minn.** ... "	7 10 We	2 20 We
12 45 Mo	1 00 Mo	679	" **Fargo, N. Dak.** .... "	2 53 We	9 35 We
4 19 Mo	4 33 Mo	873	" **Bismarck, N. Dak. (C.T.)** "	11 07 Tu	5 53 We
1 47 Tu	11 48 Mo	1319	" **Billings, Mont. (M.T.)** ... Lv	2 05 Tu	7 22 We

> Yellowstone Park Gateway
> Billings-Red Lodge — See Table 22
> Livingston-Gardiner—See Table 23

4 05 Tu	1 54 Mo	1435	Lv **Livingston, Mont.** Lv	12 01 Tu	5 05 Tu
4 50 Tu	2 39 Mo	1460	" **Bozeman** Lv	11 06 Tu	4 16 Tu
7 00 Tu	5 06 Mo	1555	Ar **Butte** Lv	8 40 Tu	1 50 Tu
7 00 Tu	4 30 Mo	1558	Ar **Helena** Lv	8 35 Tu	1 56 Tu
10 01 Tu	7 29 Mo	1675	Lv **Missoula, Mont. (M.T.)** .. "	6 13 Tu	11 17 Tu
2 09 Tu	11 27 Mo	1932	Ar **Spokane, Wash. (P.T.)** .. "	11 44 Mo	11 24 Tu
7 23 We	4 35 Mo	2158	" **Yakima**	6 49 Mo	7 15 Mo
11 45 We	8 45 Tu	2331	Ar **Seattle**	2 30 Mo	7 15 Mo
11 50 We	8 45 Tu	2328	Ar **Tacoma, Wash.** Lv	2 00 Mo	6 45 Mo
5 30 We	7 00 Tu	2317	Ar **Portland, Ore.** Lv	3 00 Mo	9 45 Mo

The Mainstreeter originates and terminates at St. Paul. Eastbound passengers continuing to Chicago may make direct platform transfer at Minneapolis to **Train 10**, The Afternoon Zephyr, leaving Minneapolis 3:55 p.m., arriving Chicago 11:15 p.m.

DENVER ZEPHYR
CHICAGO-OMAHA-DENVER

WESTBOUND—Read Down   EASTBOUND—Read Up

1 Denver Zephyr Daily	Miles	Table C	2 Denver Zephyr Daily
		Burlington Northern Inc.	
4 45	0	Lv **Chicago, Ill.** (C.T.) ...... Ar	9 50
7 20	162	" **Galesburg, Ill.** .... "	6 59
8 10	206	" **Burlington, Iowa** .... "	6 11
9 17	280	" **Ottumwa** .... "	4 58
10 56	393	" **Creston** .... "	3 20
12 45	496	Ar **Omaha, Nebr.** Lv	1 36
1 10	496	Lv **Omaha, Nebr.** .... Ar	1 26
2 10	551	Lv **Lincoln** Lv	12 29
2 30	551	Lv **Lincoln** .... Ar	12 05
4 06	648	" **Hastings** Lv	10 45
	680	" **Minden** .... "	⑱10 03
4 57	702	" **Holdrege** .... "	9 44
	726	" **Oxford** .... "	9 19
6 07	779	" **McCook, Nebr. (C.T.)** ...... "	8 34
7 06	992	" **Akron, Colo. (M.T.)** ...... "	5 37
7 35	956	" **Fort Morgan** .... "	5 05
9 00	1034	Ar **Denver** Lv	4 00
		Continental Bus	
9 05	1034	Lv ⑤**Denver** .... Ar	3 15
10 35	1109	Ar ⑤**Colorado Springs** Lv	1 45

All Space on the Denver Zephyrs is RESERVED and specifically assigned in advance. Passengers traveling from Colorado Springs should request reservations from Burlington Northern Colorado Springs office. Coach seat reservations must be claimed at train gate at Chicago by 4:35 p.m., Denver by 3:50 p.m. See page 14 for coach seat charges. Checked baggage is carried only between Chicago and Denver and not to or from intermediate points except baggage can be checked to or from unrestricted stations between Omaha and McCook.

CHICAGO-DENVER-SAN FRANCISCO
Via Burlington Northern-Rio Grande-Southern Pacific

WESTBOUND—Read Down   EASTBOUND—Read Up

15 Tri-Weekly	Miles	Table D	16 Tri-Weekly
		Burlington Northern	
11 59 Sun-Wed-Fri	0	Lv **Chicago** (C.T.) ...... Ar	8 40 Mon-Wed-Sat
2 55 Sun-Wed-Fri	162	" **Galesburg, Ill.** Lv	5 30 Mon-Wed-Sat
3 45 Sun-Wed-Fri	206	" **Burlington, Ia.** ...... "	4 05 Mon-Wed-Sat
4 57 Sun-Wed-Fri	280	" **Ottumwa** ...... "	2 40 Mon-Wed-Sat
6 41 Sun-Wed-Fri	393	" **Creston** ...... "	12 45 Mon-Wed-Sat
7 28 Sun-Wed-Fri	443	" **Red Oak** ...... "	11 45 Mon-Wed-Sat
8 45 Sun-Wed-Fri	496	Ar **Omaha, Nebr.** Lv	10 45 Mon-Wed-Sat
9 10 Sun-Wed-Fri	496	Lv **Omaha, Nebr.** ...... Ar	9 45 Mon-Wed-Sat
10 25 Sun-Wed-Fri	551	" **Lincoln, Nebr. (C.T.)** Lv	8 44 Mon-Wed-Sat
6 00 Mon-Thu-Sat	1034	Ar **Denver, Colo. (M.T.)** Lv	11 30 Sun-Tue-Fri
		Rio Grande RR	
6 30 Mon-Thu-Sat	1034	Lv **Denver** ...... Ar	11 00 Sun-Tue-Fri
8 30 Mon-Thu-Sat	1604	Ar **Salt Lake City** Lv	9 00 Sun-Tue-Fri
10 15 Mon-Thu-Sat	1640	Ar **Ogden** Lv	7 15 Sun-Tue-Fri
		(See Note)	
		Southern Pacific RR	
10 30 Mon-Thu-Sat	1640	Lv **Ogden, Utah (M.T.)** Ar	7 00 Sun-Tue-Fri
3 15 Tue-Fri-Sun	2420	" **Oakland (16th St.)** .. "	1 00 Sat-Mon-Thu
3 45 Tue-Fri-Sun	2426	Ar **San Francisco**	12 30 Sat-Mon-Thu
		(3rd Street) Lv	

Note: Passengers make cross platform transfer at Ogden.
All Space is RESERVED and specifically assigned in advance. Coach seat reservations from Chicago must be claimed at train gate by 11:50 a.m. No charge for coach seat reservations locally on BN. Extra charge applies on D&RGW of $3.75 first class and $1.50 coach. Southern Pacific charge of $10 first class and $5 coach class plus $2.25 coach seat reservation between Ogden and Oakland. Dome seats not reserved. No checked baggage between Chicago and Denver.

Schedules shown are in local prevailing time

The October 25, 1970 Burlington Northern Railroad condensed schedule is shown for the *Empire Builder–Western Star*, *North Coast Limited–Mainstreeter*, *Denver Zephyr*, and Chicago–Denver–San Francisco service. (*Beth Anne Keates collection*)

1

Burlington Northern Santa Fe Railway (BNSF Railway)

I n 1988, the Atchison, Topeka & Santa Fe Railroad showed a net loss of $46.5 million, and the company name was changed to Santa Fe Pacific Corporation (SFP) in 1989. Hard times in the rail industry produced greater cooperation between companies. SFP reached agreement with Burlington Inc. to share a rail terminal. Railway congestion around Houston, Phoenix, and South California delayed SFP deliveries resulting in declining revenues. SFP began looking for a railroad with which it could merge its operations and found Burlington a willing partner. A merger had benefits for both railroads. SFP would gain capital to stabilize its financial condition, gain access to trackage, and new customers. Burlington Northern would also gain new trackage, new shippers, more access to the petroleum belt, and a single line from British Columbia to San Diego, California. On December 31, 1996; the Atchison, Topeka and Santa Fe Railroad and Burlington Northern Railroad formally merged into the Burlington Northern Santa Fe Railway (BNSF). Chairman of the Burlington Northern, Gerald Grinstein, and president of the SFP, Robert Krebs, managed merger details in a friendly and effective manner which achieved a successful merger. Building on the foundation of BNSF's 390 predecessor railroads, this railroad serves the western two-thirds of the United States, portions of Canada, and important Mexican gateways. By the end of 1997, Burlington Northern Santa Fe Corporation—Company History noted, "Burlington Northern Santa Fe Railroad had become the largest transporter of low sulfur coal in the entire world, the largest transporter of grain throughout the United States, the largest transporter of aircraft parts, beer, and aluminum in America, and had hauled enough coal in 1997 to generate almost ten percent of the country's entire electrical output." The name was officially changed to BNSF Railway on January 24, 2005 which became a subsidiary of Berkshire Hathaway on February 12, 2010. BNSF is a vital link in the global supply chain and enables its customers to be involved in a wide range of markets in North America and around the world.

As noted by the BNSF Railway Company "Class 1 Railroad Annual Report to the Surface Transportation Board for the Year ending December 31, 2020," BNSF owned 22,855 miles of single track as follows: Alabama 105, Arizona 592, Arkansas 190, California 913, Colorado, 802, Idaho 133, Illinois 1,151, Iowa 594, Kansas 1,138, Louisiana 240, Minnesota 1,490, Mississippi 166, Missouri 1,424, Montana 2,543, Nebraska 1,477, New Mexico 1,125, North Dakota 1,552, Oklahoma 957, Oregon 226, South Dakota 864, Tennessee 16, Texas 2,596, Washington 1,334, Wisconsin 245; and Wyoming 960 plus 22 miles in British Columbia, Canada. In addition, there were 9,672 miles of single track operated under trackage rights, 40 miles operated under lease, and 31 miles operated under contract for a total mileage of 32,672.

BNSF's operating ratio (how much money has to be spent to earn a dollar of revenue with the lower the number the higher the profit) showed an improvement of 1.5 percent from 65.2 percent for the first quarter of 2020 to 63.7 percent for the first quarter of 2021. Going back to the first quarter on 2017, BNSF's operating ratio was considerable higher at 68.5 percent. BNSF net income increased 5 percent from $1.19 billion for the first quarter of 2020 to $1.252 billion for the first quarter of 2021. Total revenue decreased 0.3 percent from $5.417 billion for the first quarter of 2020 to $5.401 billion for the first quarter of 2021. According to BNSF, "The decrease was primarily due to a 5 percent increase in unit volume offset by a 5 percent decrease in average revenue per unit." Consumer products revenue increased 7 percent from $1.765 billion for the first quarter of 2020 to $1.89 billion for the first quarter of 2021. Agricultural products revenue increased 14 percent from $1.144 billion for the first quarter of 2020 to $1.308 billion for the first quarter of 2021. However, industrial products revenue decreased 16 percent from $1.465 billion for the first quarter of 2020 to $1.226 billion for the first quarter of 2021. Coal revenues decreased 10 percent from $.766 billion for the first quarter of 2020 to $.686 billion for the first quarter of 2021.

An April 21, 2022 look at the www.bnsf.com/ship website provides information on BNSF's dedicated train service where high volumes of single commodities are moved from a single origin to a single destination. The website notes that this non-stop service between a single origin and destination is, "Excellent for large volumes of single bulk commodities such as coal, grain, minerals, liquids, special project cargo, and oversized commodities such as wind blades."

Unlike other modes of transportation, United States railroads, including BNSF Railway, own, fund, build, and maintain railroad right of way. That investment includes track renewal, expanding track, technology, new freight cars and new locomotives.

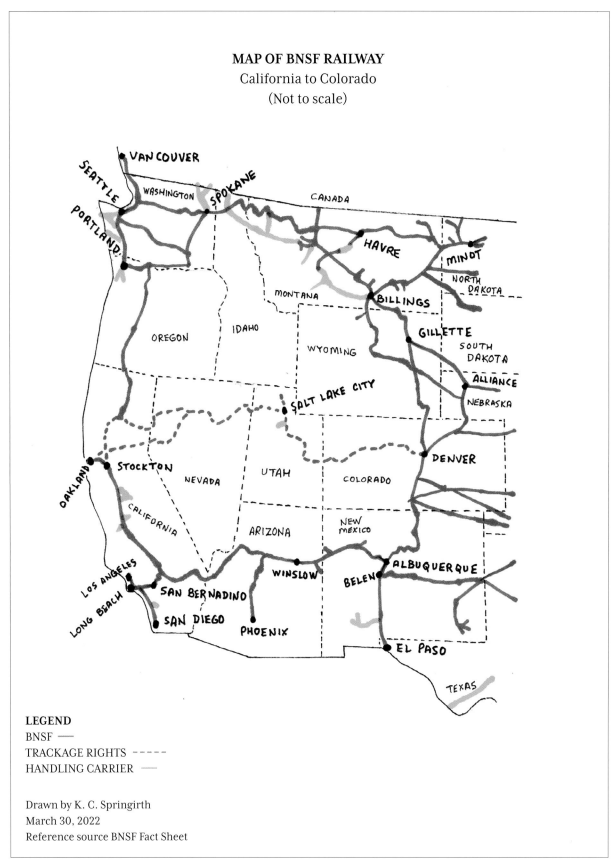

This is a map of the western portion of the Burlington Northern Santa Fe Railway. For both the western portion and eastern portion, the legend shows the handling carrier in green. Handling carrier is a railroad that works for a flat fee that is paid by either the last line haul carrier or the first line haul carrier, depending on which end the handling carrier is involved with.

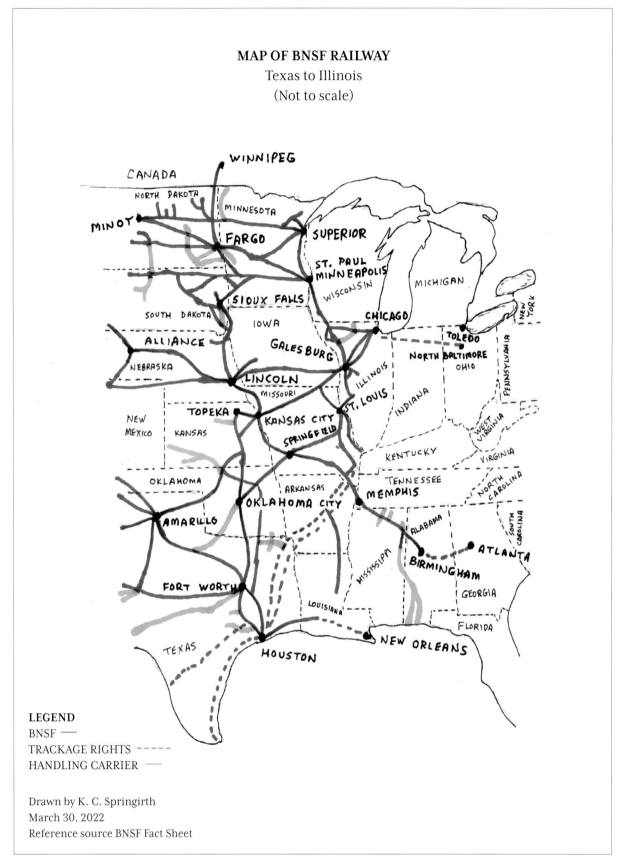

MAP OF BNSF RAILWAY
Texas to Illinois
(Not to scale)

LEGEND
BNSF ——
TRACKAGE RIGHTS - - - - -
HANDLING CARRIER ——

Drawn by K. C. Springirth
March 30, 2022
Reference source BNSF Fact Sheet

This is a map of the eastern portion of the Burlington Northern Santa Fe Railway.

On November 9, 2018, BNSF 4,300-horsepower locomotive No. 284 (type SD75I originally No. 8284 built December 1997 and rebuilt on February 21, 2018 becoming No. 284) is leading a general manifest train passing the BNSF Topeka, Kansas, Shops. The type SD75I locomotive weighs 398,000 pounds, has a top speed of 70 miles per hour, and has an "Isolated Cab" also known as a "Whisper Cab" which reduces noise and vibration in the locomotive cab. (*Jacob A. Keates photograph*)

In a Warbonnette paint scheme, BNSF locomotive No. 775 (4,400-horsepower GE designation Dash 9-44CW built in September 1997) is part of a group of locomotives powering an intermodal train past the Kansas City Union Station on August 31, 2021. This locomotive weighs 420,000 pounds and has a top speed of 73 miles per hour. (*Andrew L. Keates photograph*)

On August 31, 2021, BNSF locomotive No. 778 (GE designation Dash 9-44CW built in September 1997) is passing by the Topeka, Kansas, Amtrak Station which is close to the BNSF Topeka Shops. (*Brian A. Keates photograph*)

Topeka, Kansas, Shops finds BNSF locomotive No. 789 (GE C44-9W built in September 1997) in its former Santa Fe paint scheme waiting for the next assignment on December 12, 2019. (*Brian A. Keates photograph*)

On August 8, 2019, BNSF 1,800-horsepower locomotive No. 1503 (EMD/MK GP28-2 originally built in April 1957 as Northern Pacific No. 313 and later became Burlington Northern No. 1751) is at the BNSF Shops in Topeka, Kansas, awaiting maintenance. This locomotive was rebuilt on September 18. 1992. Also in the picture is 2,300-horsepower locomotive No. 2944 originally Santa Fe No. 3688 (EMD type GP39-2 built in May 1979). (*Brian A. Keates photograph*)

Smartly painted BNSF 3,800-horsepower locomotive No. 1424 (EMD type SD60M built in March 1990 as No. 9243 for the Burlington Northern and rebuilt on June 6, 2018) is pulling a general manifest train east bound through the Santa Fe Junction at Kansas City, Missouri, on September 2, 2021. The BNSF 1400–1476 series were renumbered from the 8109–8199 series between February and July 2014. (*Brian A. Keates photograph*)

On September 2, 2021, BNSF 3,800-horsepower locomotive No. 1438 (EMD type SD60M built in January 1991 as Burlington Northern No. 9261 and rebuilt on July 27, 2018) is trailing on a general manifest train eastbound through the Santa Fe Junction through Kansas City, Missouri. (*Brian A. Keates photograph*)

BNSF 2,300-horsepower locomotive No. 2641 (EMD type GP39-3R originally Santa Fe No. 1397 built in July 1965 and rebuilt in July 2014) is switching the shops and yard in Topeka, Kansas, on September 1, 2021. (*Brian A. Keates photograph*)

From left to right: BNSF switchers No. 2526 EMD 2,300-horsepower GP39-3Q (originally Santa Fe No. 1279 built in June 1963 and rebuilt in February 17, 2017) and No. 2728 EMD 2,300-horsepower EMD GP39-2R (originally Burlington Northern No. 2728 built in April 1981) are on a siding waiting for the next assignment on September 1, 2021. (*Brian A. Keates photograph*)

Outside of the BNSF Topeka, Kansas, Shops, BNSF 2,300-horsepower locomotive No. 2663 type GP39-3R (originally Santa Fe No. 1411 built in August 1965 and rebuilt by BNSF on October 20, 2009 at Topeka, Kansas) and No. 2835 (2,300-horsepower GP39-2 originally Santa Fe No. 3646 built in March 1975) are putting away the railroad's executive cars on October 18, 2019. (*Brian A. Keates photograph*)

On August 31, 2021, BNSF locomotive No. 3144 (originally Burlington Northern No. 3144 built in September 1985 and derated to 2,500-horsepower plus redesignated as GP25 in 2010) is one of several locomotives pulling a general manifest train through Santa Fe Junction at Kansas City, Missouri. (*Brian A. Keates photograph*)

On August 8, 2019, a group of traction motors with wheel sets are in readiness outside of the Topeka, Kansas, Shops for the next locomotive needing a motor replacement. (*Brian A. Keates photograph*)

BNSF 2,300-horsepower locomotive No. 2871 (EMD GP39-2R originally Southern Pacific No. 7452 built in February 1964) is switching cars at the BNSF Topeka, Kansas, Shops yard on December 12, 2019. (*Brian A. Keates photograph*)

The BNSF Topeka, Kansas, Shop has BNSF 2,300-horsepower locomotive No. 2944 (EMD GP39-2 originally Santa Fe No. 3688 built in May 1979) in the vintage Santa Fe yellow and blue paint scheme on August 8, 2019. (*Brian A. Keates photograph*)

Trailing on an eastbound auto train through Topeka, Kansas, on August 7, 2019, BNSF 4,400-horsepower locomotive No. 4238 (GE type ES44C4 built in January 2016) is part of 100 units Nos. 4200–4299 that were delivered during January 2016 to January 2017. This locomotive weighs 416,000 pounds and has a top speed of 73 miles per hour. (*Brian A. Keates photograph*)

On September 2, 2021, BNSF locomotive No. 4424 (GE C44-9W built in April 1999) is leading an eastbound general manifest train past the Amtrak Station at Topeka, Kansas, Station. (*Brian A. Keates photograph*)

A long BNSF train headed by locomotive No. 5043 (GE C44-9W built in July 2004) with a trailing Canadian Pacific locomotive is eastbound through the Santa Fe Junction at Kansas City, Missouri, on August 31, 2021. (*Brian A. Keates photograph*)

On August 31, 2021, the Santa Fe Junction at Kansas City, Missouri, is the location of a westbound general manifest train headed up by BNSF locomotive No. 5198 (GE C44-9W built in October 2003). (*Brian A. Keates photograph*)

On November 9, 2019, BNSF locomotive No. 5471 (GE designation Dash 9-44CW built in June 2000) is powering a grain train on the main line passing by the Topeka Shops. This was part of a group of 130 units Nos. 5370–5499 that were delivered during February to August 2000. (*Brian A. Keates photograph*)

BNSF locomotive No. 5642 (GE designation AC4400CW built in May 2003) is one of a number of locomotives on the storage track at the Topeka Shops in Topeka, Kansas, on September 1, 2021. This 4,400-horsepower locomotive weighs 420,000 pounds and has a top speed of 73 miles per hour. (*Brian A. Keates photograph*)

Awaiting the next assignment at the Topeka Shops in Topeka, Kansas, on September 1, 2021, is BNSF locomotive No. 5663 (GE AC4400CW built in January 2004). The attractive BNSF paint scheme is further enhanced by the silver wheel frames. (*Brian A. Keates photograph*)

Sitting on a display track outside of the BNSF Topeka, Kansas, Shops is BNSF locomotive No. 5777 (GE ES44AC built in August 2005) with the adjacent pond showing a reflection of a portion of the locomotive on September 3, 2021. (*Brian A. Keates photograph*)

On December 12, 2019, BNSF 4,400-horsepower locomotive No. 6376 (GE ES44AC built in November 2009) is participating in a power move at the Topeka, Kansas, Shops. (*Brian A. Keates photograph*)

Under bright skies in a locomotive power move, BNSF locomotive No. 6432 (GE ES44AC built in August 2009) is passing by the Topeka, Kansas, Shops on August 6, 2017. (*Brian A. Keates photograph*)

On August 8, 2019, BNSF locomotives No. 1503 (EMD/MK GP28-2 originally Northern Pacific No. 313 built in April 1957 and rebuilt in September 18, 1992), 6708 (GE ES44C4 built in May 2011), and 724 (GE C44-9W built in July 1997) are lined up for repairs or an overhaul at the BNSF Topeka, Kansas, Shops. (*Brian A. Keates photograph*)

The BNSF Topeka Shops on August 8, 2017 is the location for BNSF locomotives No. 2718 originally Burlington Northern No. 2718 (EMD GP39-2R built in March 1981), No. 6708 (GE ES44C4 built in May 2011), and No. 3436 (GE ET44C4 built in March 2017) awaiting repairs. (*Brian A. Keates photograph*)

On December 12, 2019, BNSF locomotive No. 6879 (GE ES44C4 built in December 2011) is involved in a power movement passing by the Topeka, Kansas, Amtrak station. (*Brian A. Keates photograph*)

BNSF locomotive No. 7071 (GE ES44C4 built in August 2012) is leading an eastbound autorack train in Topeka, Kansas. (*Brian A. Keates photograph*)

From left to right: BNSF locomotive No. 775 (GE C44-9W built in September 1997) and No. 7080 (GE ES44C4 built in August 2012) are heading an eastbound train at Union Station in Kansas City, Missouri, on August 31, 2021. (*Brian A. Keates photograph*)

On December 12, 2019, BNSF locomotive No. 7382 (GE ES44DC built in February 2010) is trailing on a BNSF intermodal westbound train on the BNSF mainline at Topeka, Kansas. (*Brian A. Keates photograph*)

BNSF locomotive No. 7856 (GE ES44DC built in April 2010) is part of four units heading an eastbound general manifest train through Topeka, Kansas, on September 2, 2021. (*Brian A. Keates photograph*)

On August 31, 2021, the Santa Fe Junction is the location of BNSF locomotive No. 8370 (GE ES44C4 built in May 2015) heading a westbound general manifest train through Kansas City, Missouri. (*Brian A. Keates photograph*)

A westbound BNSF grain train headed by 4,300-horsepower locomotive No. 8500 (EMD SD70ACe-P4 built in April 2014 by Progress Rail Services with a 16-710G3C Tier 3 engine and having a top speed of 70 miles per hour) is passing the Union Pacific Big Boy steam locomotive No. 4014 with its 4-8-8-4 wheel arrangement on tour at Union Station in Kansas City, Missouri, on August 31, 2021. The Union Pacific Railroad and BNSF share trackage at this location. (*Brian A. Keates photograph*)

On October 19, 2019, BNSF 4,000-horsepower locomotive No. 9012 (EMD SD70ACe built in October 2013) is positioned on a display track outside the Topeka Shops for "Family Day" at Topeka, Kansas. (*Brian A. Keates photograph*)

On a bright sunny December 12, 2019, BNSF locomotive No. 9202 (EMD SD70ACe built in April 2008) is at the BNSF Maintenance Facility at Topeka, Kansas. (*Brian A. Keates photograph*)

From left to right: BNSF locomotive No. 9490 (SD70MAC built in October 1994) and No. 9012 (EMD SD70ACe built in October 2013) are outside the BNSF Topeka Shops at Topeka, Kansas, on October 19, 2019. (*Brian A. Keates photograph*)

On October 19, 2019, BNSF 4,000-horsepower locomotive No. 9490 (EMD SD70MAC built in October 1994) is outside the Topeka Shops at Topeka, Kansas. This locomotive weighs 415,000 pounds and has a top speed of 70 miles per hour. (*Brian A. Keates photograph*)

In its executive paint scheme, BNSF locomotive No. 9768 (EMD SD70MAC built in May 1996) rolls west on a general manifest train via the main line through Topeka, Kansas. (*Brian A. Keates photograph*)

BNSF locomotive No. 9791 (EMD type SD70MAC built in February 1997) is powering a fully loaded coal train at North Platte, city and county seat of Lincoln County, Nebraska, on August 9, 2019. (*Andrew L. Keates photograph*)

On August 12, 2019, Citicorp Railmark Inc. (reporting mark CREX) locomotive No. 1309 GE type ES44AC is heading an intermodal train with a BNSF locomotive behind it through Topeka, Kansas. CREX is a subsidiary of Citibank (a division of Citygroup that was originally known as Citycorp Aerolease that was formed on May 13, 1970) that leases locomotives to railroads as needed. (*Brian A. Keates photograph*)

Jacob Keates, son of co-author Beth Anne Keates, graduated with honors and is shown standing erect in the second row behind the instructor (second student in from the right end of that row) with his class at the Washburn Technical School in Topeka, Kansas, on December 5, 2019. This was the last Diesel Locomotive Tech class sponsored by BNSF at this school. (*Brian A. Keates photograph*)

On August 8, 2019, this ATSF caboose No. 999714 AAR Class NE and AAR type M930 is in the yard outside of the BNSF Topeka Shops. (*Brian A. Keates photograph*)

2

Pooled Power/Run-Through Power

t is common to see a train on a railroad powered by locomotives from another railroad. An agreement between railroads to share locomotives is known as a pooled power agreement or run-through power because the locomotives run through another railroad's territory. For example, you might be at a Burlington Northern Santa Fe Railway crossing and find a train passing with Union Pacific Railway locomotives. Railroads that collaborate on run-through trains use whatever power they have in their yard. Run-through power generally does not involve monetary payments between the railroads. Compensation is based on horsepower hours. It is quicker and easier to keep the same locomotives on the train from where it starts to where it finishes. For example, railroad A receives a GP38-2 locomotive from railroad B on a run through and operates it for forty hours before returning it to railroad B. Railroad A multiples 2,000 horsepower of the GP9 by forty hours which equals 80,000 horsepower hours. Railroads keep track of horsepower hours for borrowed locomotives by taking the horsepower of the locomotive times the number of hours the locomotive worked. They owe these hours to the other railroad, and pay them back by lending their own locomotives back for an equivalent period of time. Some trains are unit trains that may start on one railroad's track and end up on another railroad to complete the trip. A locomotive due for maintenance or inspection should not be accepted in run through service unless there is an agreement addressing those issues. A railroad exchanging trains without exchanging locomotives saves both time and money.

It is also common for a railroad to lease locomotives from another company when they have a surge in traffic or when many of their locomotives are out of service. Small industrial companies might also lease a locomotive to move their railcars.

March 16, 2014, Burlington Northern Santa Fe 4,000-horsepower diesel electric locomotive No. 9116 (type SD70ACe built by the Electro-Motive Division of General Motors [EMD] in November 2012) is westbound about to cross Downing Avenue in Erie, a city in Erie County, Pennsylvania. (*Kenneth C. Springirth photograph*)

On July 29, 2019, BNSF 4,400-horsepower locomotive No. 611 (GE AC44C4M originally Santa Fe No. 611 built in February 1994 and rebuilt November 1, 2015 weighing 392,000 pounds and having a top speed of 75 miles per hour) trailing Norfolk Southern Railway locomotive No. 1040 (EMD SD70ACe placed in service on November 11, 2011) are on a westbound Norfolk Southern Railway tank train at Sinking Springs, a borough in Berks County, Pennsylvania. (*Beth Anne Keates photograph*)

On September 18, 2018, a Norfolk Southern Railway train with several BNSF locomotives including No. 615 (GE AC44C4M originally Santa FE No. 615 built in February 1994 and rebuilt on December 23, 2015) is at the Lofts at the Mill in Scranton, a city and county seat of Lackawanna County, Pennsylvania, on Delaware & Lackawanna Railroad trackage. (*Brian A. Keates photograph*)

At the former Reading Railroad Valley Forge train station (that served the Valley Forge National Historical Park near King of Prussia, Pennsylvania) that is now owned by the National Park Service and serves as a museum in Chester County, Pennsylvania, on April 30, 2022, BNSF locomotive No. 683 (GE C44-9W originally Santa Fe No. 683 built in August 1994) in a Warbonnette paint scheme is positioned waiting to pull a westbound Norfolk Southern Railway general manifest train. (*Andrew L. Keates photograph*)

On a cold rainy November 8, 2012, BNSF locomotive No. 718 (GE C44-9W built in July 1997) is at Lunenburg, a town in Worcester County, Massachusetts, on the Pan Am Railways. In July 2020, Pan Am Railways' parent Pan Am Systems was put up for sale, and CSX Transportation signed an agreement to purchase Pan Am Systems on November 30, 2020. Following review by the Surface Transportation Board, the sale was approved on April 14, 2022. (*Bob Elder photograph*)

An eastbound grain train powered by four BNSF locomotives headed by BNSF No. 736 (GE C44-9W built in August 1997) followed by No. 5675 (GE AC4400W built in February 2004) are at Fitchburg, a city in Worcester County, Massachusetts, on Pan Am Railways waiting for the incoming MBTA passenger train to arrive before continuing on to Ayer, a town in Middlesex County, Massachusetts, on April 13, 2013. (*Bob Elder photograph*)

On July 7, 2019, BNSF locomotive No. 761 (GE C44-9W built in August 1997) along with Norfolk Southern Railway locomotive No. 9736 (GE D9-44CW placed in service on December 1, 2001) are handling a westbound intermodal train on the Norfolk Southern Railway at Wyomissing, a borough in Berks County, Pennsylvania. (*Brian A. Keates photograph*)

BNSF locomotive No. 1057 (GE C44-9W built in October 1996) is trailing on a Union Pacific Railroad grain train across the Kansas River on August 9, 2019. (*Brian A. Keates photograph*)

On June 19, 2018, a Norfolk Southern Railway tank train is eastbound through Sinking Springs, Pennsylvania, with trailing locomotives Norfolk Southern Railway heritage unit No. 8103 (GE ES44AC placed in service on March 22, 2012 and painted in the Norfolk & Western Railway heritage paint scheme at the Juniata, Pennsylvania, Shops on April 9, 2012) and BNSF No. 3952 (GE ET44C4 built in August 2015). (*Brian A. Keates photograph*)

BNSF locomotive No. 4014 (GE C44-9W built in August 2003) on October 6, 2019 is leading a tank train through East Syracuse, a village and suburb of Syracuse in Onondaga County, New York, on CSX trackage. (*Brian A. Keates photograph*)

On CSX trackage, BNSF locomotive No. 4029 (GE C44-9W built in August 2003) is trailing on an empty tank train through East Syracuse, New York, on March 20, 2021. (*Brian A. Keates photograph*)

On September 19, 2014, BNSF locomotive No. 4107 (GE C44-9W built in November 2002) and No. 4611 (GE C44-9W built in December 1999) are two of the three BNSF locomotives rolling west with twenty-seven empty autorack cars at milepost 335 on Pan Am Railways (formerly) Boston & Maine Railroad at Westminster, a town in Worcester County, Massachusetts. (*Bob Elder photograph*)

On January 21, 2013, two General Electric built C44-9W locomotives No. 4108 (built in November 2002) and No. 4156 (built in September 2002) are tied down westbound on Pan Am Railways with about fifty-five BNSF-covered hopper cars at the East Fitchburg railroad yard in Lunenburg, Massachusetts. (*Bob Elder photograph*)

BNSF locomotives No. 4129 (GE C44-9W built in October 2002) and No. 4867 (GE C44-9W built in September 1998) are switching cars on Pan Am Railways at the East Fitchburg, Massachusetts, rail yard on November 8, 2012. (*Bob Elder photograph*)

On a cloudy bright August 28, 2014, Norfolk Southern Railway train No. 205 (a daily westbound empty autorack train) slowly passes on Pan Am Railways through Gardner Yard in Gardner, a city in Worcester County, Massachusetts, headed by BNSF locomotive No. 4169 (GE C44-9W built in July 2002) and trailing Norfolk Southern Railway locomotive No. 7693 (GE ES44DC placed in service on December 21, 2007). (*Bob Elder photograph*)

Pooled Power/Run-Through Power 67

An eastbound CSX grain train with trailing BNSF locomotive No. 4317 (GE C44-9W built in January 1999) is passing through Dewitt Yard in East Syracuse, New York, on November 21, 2020. (*Brian A. Keates photograph*)

On July 21, 2014, a train headed by BNSF locomotive No. 4349 (GE C44-9W built in February 1999) is waiting for a replacement crew at Watchusett Station milepost 333 on Pan Am Railways in West Fitchburg, Massachusetts. (*Bob Elder photograph*)

On March 21, 2013, BNSF locomotive No. 5111 (GE C44-9W built in May 2004) awaiting a new crew at the Willows in Ayer, Massachusetts, is powering a string of covered hopper cars on Pan Am Railways. (*Bob Elder photograph*)

On September 5, 2012, BNSF locomotive No. 5178 (GE C44-9W built in November 2003) is waiting for a clear signal at Ayer, Massachusetts, alongside Pan Am Railways locomotive No. 605 (originally built in January 1974 as Kansas City Southern 3,000-horsepower No. 660 EMD SD40-2). (*Bob Elder photograph*)

Eastbound at Altoona, a city in Blair County, Pennsylvania, over the Norfolk Southern Railway mainline on August 25, 2018, BNSF locomotive No. 5329 (GE C44-9W built in May 2001) is trailing Norfolk Southern Railway locomotive No. 9924 (GE D9-44CW placed in service on October 20, 2004). (*Brian A. Keates photograph*)

Twenty miles west of Gallitzin, Pennsylvania, near milepost 268 under a vivid blue sky on Norfolk Southern Railway's Pittsburgh Line, BNSF locomotive No. 5412 (GE C44-9W built in September 2000) is trailing Norfolk Southern Railway locomotive No. 9892 (GE D9-44CW placed in service on September 25, 2004). (*Doug Lacey, photograph*)

On March 31, 2018, BNSF locomotive No. 5493 (GE C44-9W built in May 2000) is trailing on an eastbound Norfolk Southern Railway intermodal train at Cove, an unincorporated community in Perry County, Pennsylvania. (*Brian A. Keates photograph*)

Eastbound Norfolk Southern Railway tank train headed by Norfolk Southern Railway locomotive No. 9610 (GE D9-44CW placed in service on January 27, 2001) with trailing BNSF locomotive No. 5504 (GE C44-9W built in September 2004) are passing through Cove, Pennsylvania, on April 16, 2022. (*Brian A. Keates photograph*)

On a cloudy bright November 3, 2014, BNSF locomotive No. 5946 (GE ES44AC built in April 2006) is trailing on an empty Norfolk Southern Railway empty tank train passing through Altoona, Pennsylvania. (*Brian A. Keates photograph*)

On March 7, 2020, Norfolk Southern Railway locomotive No. 1800 (rebuilt in March 2018 to type SD70ACC and repainted in a special paint scheme to highlight the conversion from DC to AC traction by Progress Rail Services of Muncie, Indiana, from NS No. 2537 type SD70 originally built by EMD in September 1994) is heading an eastbound Norfolk Southern Railway tank train in Wyomissing, Pennsylvania, with behind it BNSF trailing locomotive No. 6196 (GE type ES44AC built in February 2007). (*Brian A. Keates photograph*)

On a sunny snow-covered January 30, 2022, BNSF locomotive No. 6592 (GE ES44C4 built in April 2013) and Norfolk Southern Railway locomotive No. 4013 (originally built as No. 8782 GE D9-40C in January 1995 and rebuilt at GE Erie, Pennsylvania, as GE AC44C6M on September 26, 2016) are trailing on an eastbound Norfolk Southern Railway tank train at Brickyard crossing in Altoona, Pennsylvania. (*Brian A. Keates photograph*)

On July 7, 2018, BNSF locomotive No. 6825 (GE ES44C4 built in October 2011) is trailing on an empty westbound Norfolk Southern Railway grain train at Cove, Pennsylvania. (*Brian A. Keates photograph*)

BNSF locomotive No. 7055 (GE ES44C4 built in July 2012) is leading an eastbound CSX grain train through East Syracuse, New York, on July 5, 2021. (*Brian A. Keates photograph*)

On July 7, 2018, BNSF locomotive No. 7342 (GE ES44DC built in December 2009) and two other BNSF locomotives are trailing an empty Norfolk Southern Railway grain train through Cove, Pennsylvania. (*Brian A. Keates photograph*)

On a beautiful June 22, 2019, BNSF locomotive No. 8096 (GE ES44C4 built in March 2014) is trailing on an eastbound Norfolk Southern Railway eastbound intermodal train at Cove, Pennsylvania. (*Brian A. Keates photograph*)

An empty westbound ethanol Norfolk Southern Railway train is passing through Cove, Pennsylvania, on February 17, 2018 headed by Norfolk Southern Railway locomotive No. 9435 (GE D9-44CW placed in service on March 6, 2000) with trailing BNSF locomotive No. 8318 (GE ES44C4 built in March 2015). (*Brian A. Keates photograph*)

On March 29, 2021, Norfolk Southern Railway locomotive No. 1107 (EMD SD70ACe placed in service on February 28, 2014) is leading followed by trailing BNSF locomotive No. 7305 (GE ES44DC built in May 2009) an eastbound Norfolk Southern Railway tank train through Wyomissing, Pennsylvania. (*Brian A. Keates photograph*)

On September 19, 2021, Norfolk Southern Railway locomotive No. 7643 (GE ES44DC placed in service on April 20, 2007) is leading, and BNSF locomotive No. 6712 (GE ES44C4 built in May 2011) is trailing a westbound empty Norfolk Southern Railway empty tank train through Wyomissing, Pennsylvania. (*Brian A. Keates photograph*)

On a snow-covered March 13, 2022, Norfolk Southern Railway locomotive No. 1070 (EMD SD70ACe painted in the Wabash heritage paint scheme at Muncie, Indiana, and placed in service on June 27, 2012) is leading, and BNSF locomotive No. 6957 (GE ES44C4 built in March 2012) is trailing an eastbound Norfolk Southern Railway intermodal train through the National Park, Valley Forge Pennsylvania. (*Brian A. Keates photograph*)

Norfolk Southern Railway locomotive No. 8102 (GE ES44AC painted in the Pennsylvania Railroad heritage paint scheme at Juniata, Pennsylvania, on April 18, 2012) with a trailing BNSF locomotive plus another locomotive are powering a Norfolk Southern Railway train at Gladwyn, a suburban community in Montgomery County, Pennsylvania, on December 30, 2020. (*Doug Lacey photograph*)

On February 15, 2019 (*from left to right*), there are three trailing locomotives Norfolk Southern Railway locomotive No. 7569 (GE ES44DC placed in service on June 16, 2006) plus BNSF locomotive No. 6908 (GE ES44C4 built in January 2012), and BNSF locomotive No. 6545 (GE ES44C4 built in February 2013) on a Norfolk Southern Railway train at Cove, Pennsylvania. (*Brian A. Keates photograph*)

BNSF locomotive No. 7248 (GE ES44DC built in February 2009) is passing mile post 329.7 over a Pan Am Railways' snow-covered right of way at Fitchburg, Massachusetts, on February 15, 2013. (*Bob Elder photograph*)

On February 15, 2013, BNSF locomotive No. 7248 (GE ES44DC built in February 2009) is gliding downgrade with oil cars in tow heading a Pan Am Railways' train to Fitchburg, Massachusetts. (*Bob Elder photograph*)

A week later on February 22, 2013, BNSF locomotive No. 7248 shown in the top picture is one of three trailing BNSF locomotives passing westbound on the Pan Am Railways by a former Boston & Maine Railroad freight house. The Otter River passenger station was located across the tracks from this location in Templeton, a town in Worcester County, Massachusetts. (*Bob Elder photograph*)

BNSF locomotive No. 7355 (GE ES44DC built in December 2009) is trailing eastbound on a Norfolk Southern Railway intermodal train on August 26, 2018 over the Horseshoe Curve near Altoona, Pennsylvania. (*Brian A. Keates photograph*)

Milepost 245 on the Harrisburg, Pennsylvania, line is the location of BNSF locomotive No. 7717 (GE ES44DC built in March 2005) leading a Norfolk Southern Railway train. (*Doug Lacey photograph*)

On a cold April 1, 2022, with a dusting of snow on the ground, a westbound Norfolk Southern Railway intermodal train is approaching the Lewistown, a borough and county seat of Mifflin County, Pennsylvania, Amtrak train station headed by Norfolk Southern Railway locomotive No. 8108 (GE ES44AC placed in service on March 20, 2012) with trailing BNSF locomotive No. 7555 (GE ES44DC built in May 2007). (*Kenneth C. Springirth photograph*)

An eastbound CSX grain train on November 21, 2021, is headed by BNSF locomotive No. 8157 (GE ES44C4 built in October 2014) with another BNSF locomotive behind it on the CSX main line at Dewitt Yard at East Syracuse, New York. The "Thank You Railroaders" sign was hand painted by Beth Anne Keates, the co-author of this book. (*Brian A. Keates photograph*)

On July 1, 2021, at the Harrisburg Line milepost 24.5, Norfolk Southern Railway locomotive No. 1197 (EMD SD70ACe built in February 2019) is leading a Norfolk Southern Railway train with trailing BNSF locomotive No. 8173 (GE ES44C4 built in October 2014). (*Doug Lacey photograph*)

An eastbound Norfolk Southern Railway intermodal train is passing Wyomissing Junction on May 1, 2022 headed by Norfolk Southern Railway locomotive No. 4120 (originally No. 8883 GE D9-40C built in March 1995 and rebuilt at the Norfolk Southern Roanoke Locomotive Shop in April 2018 as GE AC44C6M) with trailing BNSF locomotive No. 8213 (GE ES44C4 built in March 2014). (*Brian A. Keates photograph*)

Trailing BNSF locomotive No. 8284 (GE ES44C4 built in July 2014) is on a Norfolk Southern Railway westbound intermodal train passing Norfolk Southern Railway track workers on April 29, 2022 at Lewistown Junction, Pennsylvania. (*Brian A. Keates photograph*)

On March 10, 2021, BNSF locomotive No. 8387 (GE ES44C4 built in May 2015) is trailing on an eastbound Norfolk Southern Railway tank train passing through Cove, Pennsylvania. (*Brian A. Keates photograph*)

3

BNSF Passes by Gallitzin's Tunnel Inn

Gallitzin, named for Prince Demetrius Augustine Gallitzin, became Gallitzin Borough on December 2, 1873, and became a railroad town 12 miles west of Altoona. At its peak, the borough of Gallitzin in Cambria County, Pennsylvania, had a population of 3,618 in 1940. Gallitzin's population has declined 57.6 percent to an estimated 1,534 in 2019. *Early History of Gallitzin* by F. J. Parrish noted, "The great famine in Ireland in 1849 which almost depopulated the Island brought thousands of noble, honest men to seek a home in the United States." He continued, "The laborers employed in and about the tunnel were, with few exceptions, Irishmen." According to Irene Snyzal, president of the Tunnels Park & Museum, resident of Gallitzin since 1941, and volunteer at the museum since 1987, "The railroad made the town. We were self sufficient, everything that you could possible need was right in Gallitzin which is a very walkable town. The Victoria Theater was immediately next to the current Tunnel Inn." At the museum, Snyzal remembered the Pennsylvania Railroad caboose, built in

1942 at the Juniata Shops in Altoona was donated and arrived at the museum in Conrail Blue. Joe Boche paid for a crane which set the caboose on newly laid track at the museum. Snyzal noted there were Bituminous coal mines all around Gallitzin and much of the fill from the tunnels was used to fill out the Horseshoe Curve area.

The high grade of the Allegheny Mountains made it necessary to build tunnels. In 1854, the 3,612-foot-long Summit Tunnel was completed at an elevation of 2,167 feet above sea level and later became known as the Allegheny Tunnel. In 1855, the New Portage Railroad Tunnel was completed by the Commonwealth of Pennsylvania. It was purchased by the Pennsylvania Railroad in 1857 and has been primarily used for eastbound traffic. During 1904, the Gallitzin Tunnel was completed north of the Allegheny Tunnel. It was removed from service when the Allegheny Tunnel was expanded to two tracks plus enlarged for double-stack rail transport for both tracks in 1995.

On April 20, 2018, BNSF locomotive No. 716 (GE C44-9W built in July 1997 in its Santa Fe war bonnet paint scheme) is trailing on an eastbound Norfolk Southern Railway freight train at milepost 248 under the Jackson Street bridge in Gallitzin, Pennsylvania. (*Bob Elder photograph*)

BNSF locomotive No. 3252 (GE ES44C4 built in first quarter of 2020) is trailing west on a Norfolk Southern Railway freight train on track three at Gallitzin, Pennsylvania, on March 13, 2021. (*Bob Elder photograph*)

On October 13, 2021, BNSF locomotive No. 4198 (GE C44-9W built in May 2002) is trailing on an eastbound Norfolk Southern Railway freight train about to enter the Allegheny Tunnel at milepost 248 in Gallitzin, Pennsylvania. In the upper left hand corner of the picture is former Pennsylvania Railroad caboose No. 477852, AAR type M930, PRR class N5C, built in June 1942, and is on display at the Tunnels Park and Museum. (*Bob Elder photograph*)

With traces of snow on the ground, a westbound Norfolk Southern Railway intermodal train headed by locomotive No. 4448 (originally No. 9136 GE D9-44CW built in February 1998 and rebuilt as GE AC44C6M at Wabtec/GE Fort Worth, Texas, in May 2021) with trailing BNSF locomotive No. 4988 (GE C44-9W built in December 1998) has emerged from the Allegheny Tunnel past the historic Tunnel Inn property on the bottom right portion of the picture at Gallitzin, Pennsylvania, on February 18, 2022. (*Brian A. Keates photograph*)

Passing under the evening lights at the Tunnel Inn on March 23, 2022, is BNSF locomotive No. 5424 (GE C44-9W built in September 2000). Note the bottom step of the Norfolk Southern Railway locomotive is illuminated. (*Bob Elder photograph*)

Trailing west through Gallitzin, Pennsylvania, past the Jackson Street bridge on the Norfolk Southern Railway are BNSF locomotives No. 3938 (GE ET44C4 built in July 2015) and No. 5448 (GE C44-9W built in July 2000). (*Doug Lacey photograph*)

On May 5, 2021, BNSF locomotive No. 5804 (GE ES44AC built in September 2005) is trailing on a Norfolk Southern Railway freight train passing by the stylish blue 1968 Chevrolet C10 pickup truck that was advertised for its smooth ride, coil springs, and easy handling (owned by Bob Elder, the inn keeper of the Tunnel Inn) parked in the parking lot of the Tunnel Inn in Gallitzin, Pennsylvania. (*Bob Elder photograph*)

Looking from the back deck of the Tunnel Inn at Milepost 248 in Gallitzin, Pennsylvania, on February 14, 2022 with a fresh blanket of snow on the ground, BNSF locomotive No. 6592 (GE ES44C4 built in April 2013) is trailing behind a Norfolk Southern Railway locomotive that is close to entering the Allegheny Tunnel. On the upper left corner of the picture is the former Pennsylvania Railroad caboose at the Gallitzin Tunnels Park and Museum. (*Bob Elder photograph*)

On a beautiful September 25, 2021, eastbound trailing BNSF locomotive No. 6838 (GE ES44C4 built in November 2011) and another BNSF locomotive on a Norfolk Southern Railway freight train are passing under the Jackson Street bridge in Gallitzin. Pennsylvania. (*Bob Elder photograph*)

Under the lighting at the Tunnel Inn in Gallitzin, Pennsylvania, BNSF locomotive No. 7006 (GE ES44C4 built in April 2012) shows up on an evening February 14, 2001 Norfolk Southern Railway intermodal train. (*Bob Elder photograph*)

On March 22, 2022, a westbound Norfolk Southern Railway train is emerging from the Allegheny Tunnel with trailing BNSF locomotive No. 7063 (GE ES44C4 built in July 2012) in Gallitzin, Pennsylvania. (*Bob Elder photograph*)

Norfolk Southern Railway freight train is parallel and adjacent to the hillside of the Tunnel Inn at Gallitzin, Pennsylvania, on August 30, 2021 with trailing BNSF locomotive No. 7112 (GE ES44C4 built in March 2013) behind Norfolk Southern Railway locomotive No. 7643 (GE ES44DC placed in service on April 20, 2007). (*Bob Elder photograph*)

On December 1, 2021, looking down the cliff from the Tunnel Inn in Gallitzin, Pennsylvania, trailing BNSF locomotive No. 7526 (GE ES44DC built in April 2007) is passing by on a Norfolk Southern Railway train at milepost 248 on the Norfolk Southern Railway's Pittsburgh Line. (*Bob Elder photograph*)

On a snow-covered March 9, 2022, a passing Norfolk Southern Railway freight train has a somewhat damaged front end on trailing westbound BNSF locomotive No. 7555 (GE ES44DC built in May 2007) at Gallitzin, Pennsylvania. (*Bob Elder photograph*)

A November 14, 2021 view looking down from the Tunnel Inn at Gallitzin, Pennsylvania, shows a Norfolk Southern Railway freight train with trailing BNSF locomotive No. 7688 (GE ES44DC built in February 2005) and Norfolk Southern Railway locomotive No. 1100 (EMD SD70ACe placed in service on February 28, 2014). (*Bob Elder photograph*)

A westbound Norfolk Southern Railway intermodal freight train headed by Norfolk Southern Railway locomotive No. 4440 (originally No. 9236 GE D9-44CW built in May 1998 and rebuilt as GE AC44C6M in March 2021 at Wabtec/GE Ft. Worth, Texas) with trailing BNSF locomotive No. 7773 (GE ES44DC built in June 2005) on November 21, 2021 have emerged from the Allegheny Tunnel and are traveling past the Tunnel Inn in Gallitzin, Pennsylvania. (*Brian A. Keates photograph*)

On February 16, 2019, trailing BNSF locomotive No. 7785 (GE ES44DC built in June 2005) along with the other eastbound locomotives on a Norfolk Southern Railway freight train are dashing through the snow passing under the Jackson Street bridge in Gallitzin, Pennsylvania. (*Bob Elder photograph*)

BNSF locomotive No. 8114 (GE ES44C4 built in July 2014) is trailing east into the 3,605-foot-long Allegheny Tunnel on March 15, 2021 at milepost 248 in Gallitzin, Pennsylvania, on a Norfolk Southern Railway freight train behind Norfolk Southern Railway 4,500-horsepower locomotive No. 7265 (EMD SD70ACU [originally Union Pacific Railroad No. 8037 EMD type SD9043MAC built in August 1996] rebuilt May 3, 2016 at the Juniata Shop). The closed tunnel in the center of the picture is the former Gallitzin Tunnel that was completed in 1904 and removed from service when the Allegheny Tunnel was expanded to two tracks in 1995. (*Bob Elder photograph*)

On a June 21, 2021 Norfolk Southern Railway freight train, BNSF locomotive No. 8173 (GE ES44C4 built in October 2014) is trailing Norfolk Southern Railway locomotive No. 1197 (EMD SD70ACe built in February 2019) at Gallitzin, Pennsylvania. (*Bob Elder photograph*)

BNSF locomotive No. 8332 (GE ES44C4 built in March 2015) is trailing on a November 21, 2021 westbound Norfolk Southern Railway intermodal train that is emerging from the Allegheny Tunnel at Gallitzin, Pennsylvania. (*Bob Elder photograph*)

On May 10, 2021, BNSF locomotive No. 8334 (GE ES44C4 built in March 2015) is on a westbound Norfolk Southern Railway freight train at milepost 248 in Gallitzin, Pennsylvania. (*Bob Elder photograph*)

BNSF locomotives No. 8340 (GE ES44C4 built in April 2015) and No. 7960 (GE ES44C4 built in January 2015) are assisting an eastbound Norfolk Southern Railway intermodal train passing under the Jackson Street bridge and heading for the Allegheny Tunnel on November 1, 2021. (*Bob Elder photograph*)

On May 5, 2021, Norfolk Southern Railway locomotive No. 9735 (GE D9-44CW placed in service on December 1, 2001) and BNSF locomotive No. 9749 (originally EMD SD70MAC built in March 1996 and rebuilt as EMD SD70MACE on September 29, 2016) are powering a Norfolk Southern Railway freight train just east of the Jackson Street bridge in Gallitzin, Pennsylvania. The "Thank You Railroaders" sign was hand painted by the co-author of this book Beth Anne Keates. (*Bob Elder photograph*)

4

Metra BNSF Chicago to Aurora, Illinois, Commuter Line

The BNSF Railway operates the 37.5-mile Metra commuter line from Union Station in Chicago to Aurora, Illinois, and the line also handles Amtrak trains and BNSF freight trains. This started as the Aurora Branch Railroad which became the Chicago and Aurora Railroad in 1852; Chicago, Burlington & Quincy Railroad (CB&Q) in 1856; on March 2, 1970 merged to form the Burlington Northern Railroad; on September 22, 1995 merged with the Atchison, Topeka & Santa Fe Railway to form the Burlington Northern Santa Fe Railway; which on January 24, 2005, the name was shortened to BNSF Railway. The Regional Transportation Authority (RTA) began subsidizing Chicago's commuter rail operations in 1974, and the Burlington Northern Railroad continued to operate its line under contract to the RTA. This continued under Metra.

Freight trains carried milk, hay, and wheat to Chicago from small agricultural towns such as Naperville, Downers Grove, Hinsdale, and La Grange. Early suburban trains on this line had wooden open ended coaches pulled by 4-4-0 steam locomotives. As ridership grew, trains became longer and train speeds increased, larger steam locomotives such as Ten Wheelers with a 4-6-0 wheel arrangement were placed in service. By 1930, steel passenger cars replaced the wooden passenger cars. In 1934, this line hosted the stainless-steel, diesel-powered *Zephyr*. While the *Zephyrs* never powered suburban commuter trains, during 1949, diesel electric locomotives began to replace steam locomotives, and in 1952 Chicago–Aurora commuter service was completely dieselized. In 1950, new 85-foot-long, bi-level, stainless, air-conditioned, roller-bearing commuter cars with a seating capacity of 148 passengers per car were built by the Budd Company of Philadelphia for the Chicago–Aurora line. This was the first railroad in Chicago to use stainless steel, bi-level air-conditioned commuter cars.   These cars handled more riders which expanded capacity without the need for more trains and longer trains. By 1965, Chicago–Aurora commuter service was completely converted to the new bi-level cars. In 1964–1965, a push-pull train was introduced which does not require turning at the end of the line. A group of bi-level cars were modified to have operating controls at one end, so that the train can be manned from either the engine, in one direction or from the last car in the other direction.

Over the years, the western suburbs served by this line grew up with the railroad, and the railroad grew with the suburbs. The Burlington Northern Railroad (BN) was formed by the March 2, 1970 merger of the Great Northern Railway; Northern Pacific Railway; Spokane, Portland & Seattle Railway; and the Chicago, Burlington & Quincy Railroad. In 1972, the West Suburban Mass Transit District was formed by communities along the line to help BN secure funding for capital improvements for the line. Area voters approved the creation of the Regional Transportation Authority (RTA) to assist public transportation in 1973, and the RTA Act was amended in 1983 to place commuter rail under newly formed Commuter Rail Division which became known as Metra in 1985. Metra owns all of the commuter rail rolling stock, is responsible for most of the stations, controls fares, and staffing levels.

On December 31, 1996, the Burlington Northern Santa Fe Railway resulted from the merger of the Atchison, Topeka & Santa Fe Railway with the Burlington Northern Railroad, and the name was shortened to BNSF Railway. BNSF operates the commuter line with its own crews and controls the right of way under a purchase of service agreement with Metra. For the year ending December 1, 2020, Metra paid BNSF $7,334,065 for diesel fuel, $3,096,874 for claims and insurance, and $7,558,238 for downtown stations or a total of $17,989,177.

Annual ridership on the BNSF commuter line has declined 7.15 percent from 16,658,357 in 2014 to 15,468,014 in 2019. However, as a result of the COVID-19 pandemic, one year later ridership declined 76.34 percent to 3,659,617 in 2020. There was a further decline to 2,483,782 in 2021 according to the Metra 2021 Annual Report (Updated March 2022). This line continues to have the highest ridership of the 11 Metra lines. According to the Eno Center for Transportation, "Commuter rail riders are generally wealthier than other transit users, work traditional business hours, and can more easily shift to working from home." Hence it may be more difficult for that BNSF commuter line to recover. The Commuter Rail Division of the Regional Transportation Authority and the Northeast Illinois Regional Commuter Railroad Corporation December 31, 2020 noted, "Prior to COVID-19 approximately 90 percent of passenger trips taken on Metra were for work." That report noted, "Passenger revenue decreased 72 percent from $365.9 million in 2019 to $102.4 million in 2020." On the positive side, the report noted Metra's "on-time performance reached 96.5 percent in 2020, an increase from 94.6 percent in 2019." Metra has an extensive program for in house rehabilitation of cars and locomotives plus locomotives are also remanufactured by external suppliers.

The March 28, 2022 weekday schedule showed thirty-two trips from Aurora to Chicago and thirty-four trips from Chicago to Aurora. Off peak service was hourly. There were additional trips between Fairview and Chicago plus between Brookfield and Chicago during the morning and afternoon peak period. Saturday passenger service was mostly hourly except for two express trips from Aurora to Chicago and one express trip from Chicago to Aurora. Sunday service was every two hours and trips on both Saturday and Sunday had a bike car.

AURORA to CHICAGO – Monday through Friday

♿	Zone	Station	1200 AM	1202 AM	1206 AM	1204 AM	1208 AM	1210 AM	1212 AM	1214 AM	1216 AM	1218 AM	1220 AM	1222 AM	1306 AM	1224 AM	1226 AM	1228 AM	1230 AM	1232 AM	1234 AM	1236 AM
•	H	Aurora LV	4:00	4:29	5:02			5:32	5:29		6:02			6:32	6:47	6:29		7:02	7:17			7:32
•	G	Route 59	4:08	4:36	5:11			5:41	5:36		6:11			6:41	6:56	6:36		7:11	7:26			7:41
•	F	Naperville	4:13	4:41	5:17			5:47	5:41		6:17			6:47	7:02	6:41		7:17	7:32			7:47
•	E	Lisle	4:19	4:47	5:23			5:53	5:47		6:23			6:53	---	6:47		7:23	---			7:53
•	E	Belmont	4:22	4:50	5:26			5:56	5:50		6:26			6:56	---	6:50		7:26	---			7:56
•	E	Downers Grv./Main St.	4:26	4:53	5:30			6:00	5:53		6:30			7:00	---	6:53		7:30	---			8:00
•	E	Fairview Ave.	4:29	4:55	---	5:18	5:42	---	5:55	6:12	---		6:42	---	---	6:55	7:12	---	---		7:42	---
•	D	Westmont	4:31	4:57	---	5:20	5:44	---	5:57	6:14	---		6:44	---	---	6:57	7:14	---	---		7:44	---
○	D	Clarendon Hills	4:34	5:00	---	5:23	5:47	---	6:00	6:17	---		6:47	---	---	7:00	7:17	---	---		7:47	---
•	D	West Hinsdale	4:36	5:02	---	5:25	5:49	---	6:02	6:19	---		6:49	---	---	7:02	7:19	---	---		7:49	---
•	D	Hinsdale	4:38	5:05	---	5:27	5:52	---	6:05	6:22	---		6:52	---	---	7:05	7:22	---	---		7:52	---
•	D	Highlands	4:40	5:07	---	5:30	5:54	---	6:07	6:24	---		6:54	---	---	7:07	7:24	---	---		7:54	---
•	D	Western Springs	4:43	5:09	---	5:33	5:57	---	6:09	6:27	---		6:57	---	---	7:09	7:27	---	---		7:57	---
•	C	LaGrange, Stone Ave.	4:46	5:13	---	5:36	6:00	---	6:13	6:30	---		7:00	---	---	7:13	7:30	---	---		8:00	---
	C	LaGrange Rd.	4:48	5:15	---	5:38	6:02	---	6:15	6:32	---		7:02	---	---	7:15	7:32	---	---		8:02	---
	C	Congress Park	4:51	5:17	---	5:40	6:05	---	6:17	6:35	---		7:05	---	---	7:17	7:35	---	---		8:05	---
○	C	Brookfield	---	5:19	---	5:42	---	---	6:19	---	---	6:51	---	---	---	7:19	---	---	---	7:51	---	---
•	C	Hollywood (Zoo Stop)	---	5:21	---	5:44	---	---	6:21	---	---	6:53	---	---	---	7:21	---	---	---	7:53	---	---
○	C	Riverside	---	5:24	---	5:47	---	---	6:24	---	---	6:56	---	---	---	7:24	---	---	---	7:56	---	---
•	B	Harlem Ave.	---	5:27	---	5:50	---	---	6:27	---	---	6:59	---	---	---	7:27	---	---	---	7:59	---	---
•	B	Berwyn	---	5:29	---	5:52	---	---	6:29	---	---	7:01	---	---	---	7:29	---	---	---	8:01	---	---
•	B	LaVergne	---	5:30	---	5:53	---	---	6:30	---	---	7:02	---	---	---	7:30	---	---	---	8:02	---	---
•	B	Cicero	---	5:35	---	5:58	---	---	6:35	---	---	7:07	---	---	---	7:35	---	---	---	8:07	---	---
	A	Western Ave.	---	5:40	---	6:03	---	---	6:40	---	---	7:12	---	---	---	7:40	---	---	---	8:12	---	---
	A	Halsted St.	---	5:43	---	6:06	---	---	6:43	---	---	7:15	---	---	---	7:43	---	---	---	8:15	---	---
•	A	Chicago CUS AR	5:12	5:52	6:00	6:15	6:26	6:30	6:52	6:56	7:00	7:22	7:26	7:30	7:41	7:52	7:56	8:00	8:11	8:22	8:26	8:30
		# of bikes allowed per train	10	10	10	10	5	5														

▲ subject to construction

CHICAGO to AURORA – Monday through Friday

♿	Zone	Station	1201 AM	1203 AM	1205 AM	1207 AM	1211 AM	1213 AM	1215 AM	1217 AM	1221 AM	1223 AM	1225 AM	1227 AM	1229 PM	1231 PM	1301 PM	1233 PM	1235 PM	1239 PM	1241 PM	1243 PM	1245 PM
•	A	Chicago CUS LV	5:35	6:05	6:20	6:25	6:47	7:05	7:15	7:33	8:33	9:33	10:33	11:33	12:33	1:33	2:30	2:33	3:00	3:10	3:30	3:35	3:40
	A	Halsted St.	5:42	6:11	---	6:31	6:53	7:11	7:21	7:39	8:39	9:39	10:39	11:39	12:39	1:39	---	2:39	---	3:15	---	---	3:45
	A	Western Ave.	5:46	6:15	6:28	6:35	6:57	7:15	7:25	7:43	8:43	9:43	10:43	11:43	12:43	1:43	---	2:43	---	3:19	---	---	3:49
•	B	Cicero	5:51	6:20	6:34	6:40	7:03	7:20	7:31	7:48	8:48	9:48	10:48	11:48	12:48	1:48	---	2:48	---	3:24	---	---	3:54
•	B	LaVergne	---	6:24	---	6:44	---	7:24	---	---	---	---	---	---	---	---	---	---	---	3:28	---	---	3:58
•	B	Berwyn	5:55	6:26	---	6:46	---	7:26	---	7:53	8:53	9:53	10:53	11:53	12:53	1:53	---	2:53	---	3:30	---	---	4:00
•	B	Harlem Ave.	5:57	6:28	---	6:48	---	7:28	---	7:55	8:55	9:55	10:55	11:55	12:55	1:55	---	2:55	---	3:32	---	---	4:02
○	C	Riverside	6:00	6:30	---	6:50	---	7:30	---	7:57	8:57	9:57	10:57	11:57	12:57	1:57	---	2:57	---	3:34	---	---	4:04
•	C	Hollywood (Zoo Stop)	---	6:33	---	6:53	---	7:33	---	---	---	---	---	---	---	---	---	---	---	3:37	---	---	4:07
○	C	Brookfield	6:04	6:35	---	6:55	---	7:35	7:38	8:00	9:00	10:00	11:00	12:00	1:00	2:00	---	3:00	---	3:39	---	---	4:10
	C	Congress Park	---		---	---	---		---	---	---	---	---	---	---	---	---	---	---	3:41	---	3:52	
•	C	LaGrange Rd.	6:07		---	6:58	7:12		7:42	8:04	9:04	10:04	11:04	12:04	1:04	2:04	---	3:04	---	3:43	---	3:55	
•	C	LaGrange, Stone Ave.	---		---	---	---		---	---	---	---	---	---	---	---	---	---	---	3:45	---	3:57	
•	D	Western Springs	6:11		---	7:02	---		---	8:08	9:08	10:08	11:08	12:08	1:08	2:08	---	3:08	---	3:48	---	4:00	
•	D	Highlands	---		---	---	---		---	---	---	---	---	---	---	---	---	---	---	3:51	---	4:03	
•	D	Hinsdale	6:14		---	7:05	---		---	8:11	9:11	10:11	11:11	12:11	1:11	2:11	---	3:11	---	3:53	---	4:05	
•	D	West Hinsdale	---		---	---	---		---	---	---	---	---	---	---	---	---	---	---	3:56	---	4:08	
○	D	Clarendon Hills	6:18		---	7:09	---		---	8:15	9:15	10:15	11:15	12:15	1:15	2:15	---	3:15	---	3:58	---	4:10	
•	D	Westmont	6:21		---	7:13	---		7:51	8:18	9:18	10:18	11:18	12:18	1:18	2:18	---	3:18	---	4:01	---	4:13	
•	E	Fairview Ave.	---		---	7:16	7:20		7:54	---	---	---	---	---	---	---	---	---	---	4:04	---	4:17	
•	E	Downers Grv./Main St	6:24		6:50		7:22			8:22	9:22	10:22	11:22	12:22	1:22	2:22	2:56	3:22	3:26	4:06	3:56		
•	E	Belmont	6:27		6:54		7:25			8:25	9:25	10:25	11:25	12:25	1:25	2:25	3:00	3:25	3:28	4:09	4:00		
•	E	Lisle	6:31		6:57		7:29			8:28	9:28	10:28	11:28	12:28	1:28	2:28	3:03	3:28	3:33	4:12	4:03		
•	F	Naperville	6:37		7:04		7:36			8:34	9:34	10:34	11:34	12:34	1:34	2:34	3:08	3:34	3:38	4:18	4:08		
•	G	Route 59	6:41		7:09		7:41			8:38	9:38	10:38	11:38	12:38	1:38	2:38	3:13	3:38	3:43	4:23	4:13		
•	H	Aurora AR	6:54		7:21		7:51			8:50	9:50	10:50	11:50	12:50	1:50	2:50	3:27	3:50	3:57	4:35	4:27		
		# of bikes allowed per train	10	10	10	10	10	10	10	10	10	10	10	10	10	10	10						

▲ subject to construction

♿ = ADA Accessibility: • = ADA Accessible Station   ○ = Partially ADA Accessible Station – station meets some, but not all ADA requirements. | ▲ = Trains may be su[bject]...

The Metra BNSF March 28, 2022 top portion of the schedule shows an extensive amount of passenger service in the Monday through Friday morning rush hour service from Aurora to Chicago, Illinois. Monday through Friday bottom portion of the schedule from Chicago to Aurora shows express trips that arrive at Aurora in a timely manner to enhance service morning rush hour service back to Chicago. This page shows about half of the service and page 97 shows the remainder.

1242 AM	1244 AM	1246 AM	1304 AM	1250 AM	1252 AM	1254 AM	1256 AM	1258 PM	1260 PM	1262 PM	1264 PM	1268 PM	1272 PM	1274 PM	1276 PM	1282 PM	1284 PM	1292 PM	1294 PM	1296 PM	1298 PM	1300 PM	1302 PM
7:29		8:02		8:32	9:04	10:04	11:04	12:04	1:04	2:04	3:04	3:40	4:07		4:37		5:04	6:04	7:04	8:04	9:04	10:04	11:04
7:36		8:11		8:41	9:11	10:11	11:11	12:11	1:11	2:11	3:11	3:47	4:14		4:44		5:11	6:11	7:11	8:11	9:11	10:11	11:11
7:41		8:17		8:47	9:15	10:15	11:15	12:15	1:15	2:15	3:15	3:51	4:19		4:49		5:15	6:15	7:15	8:15	9:15	10:15	11:15
7:47		8:23		8:53	9:21	10:21	11:21	12:21	1:21	2:21	3:21	3:57	4:24		4:54		5:21	6:21	7:21	8:21	9:21	10:21	11:21
7:50		8:26		8:56	9:24	10:24	11:24	12:24	1:24	2:24	3:24	4:00	4:27		4:57		5:24	6:24	7:24	8:24	9:24	10:24	11:24
7:53		8:30	8:40	9:00	9:27	10:27	11:27	12:27	1:27	2:27	3:27	4:06	4:31		5:01		5:27	6:27	7:27	8:27	9:27	10:27	11:27
7:55	8:12	---	8:42	---	---	---	---	---	---	---	---	---	4:34	4:39	5:04	5:09	---	---	---	---	---	---	---
7:57	8:14	---	8:44	---	9:31	10:31	11:31	12:31	1:31	2:31	3:31	4:10	---	4:41	---	5:11	5:31	6:31	7:31	8:31	9:31	10:31	11:31
8:00	8:17	---	8:47	---	9:34	10:34	11:34	12:34	1:34	2:34	3:34	4:13	---	4:44	---	5:14	5:34	6:34	7:34	8:34	9:34	10:34	11:34
8:02	8:19	---	8:49	---	---	---	---	---	---	---	---	---	---	---	---	---	---	---	---	---	---	---	---
8:05	8:22	---	8:52	---	9:37	10:37	11:37	12:37	1:37	2:37	3:37	4:17	---	4:48	---	5:18	5:37	6:37	7:37	8:37	9:37	10:37	11:37
8:07	8:24	---	8:55	---	---	---	---	---	---	---	---	---	---	---	---	---	---	---	---	---	---	---	---
8:09	8:27	---	8:58	---	9:40	10:40	11:40	12:40	1:40	2:40	3:40	4:20	---	4:51	---	5:21	5:40	6:40	7:40	8:40	9:40	10:40	11:40
8:13	8:30	---	9:01	---	---	---	---	---	---	---	---	---	---	---	---	---	---	---	---	---	---	---	---
8:15	8:32	---	9:03	---	9:43	10:43	11:43	12:43	1:43	2:43	3:43	4:24	4:42	4:55	---	5:25	5:43	6:43	7:43	8:43	9:43	10:43	11:43
8:17	8:35	---	9:05	---	---	---	---	---	---	---	---	---	---	---	---	---	---	---	---	---	---	---	---
8:19	---	---	9:07	---	9:47	10:47	11:47	12:47	1:47	2:47	3:47	4:28	---	4:59	---	5:29	5:47	6:47	7:47	8:47	9:47	10:47	11:47
8:21	---	---	9:09	---	---	---	---	---	---	---	---	---	---	5:01	---	5:31	---	---	---	---	---	---	---
8:24	---	---	9:12	---	9:50	10:50	11:50	12:50	1:50	2:50	3:50	4:31	---	5:04	---	5:34	5:50	6:50	7:50	8:50	9:50	10:50	11:50
8:27	---	---	9:15	---	9:52	10:52	11:52	12:52	1:52	2:52	3:52	4:34	---	5:07	---	5:37	5:52	6:52	7:52	8:52	9:52	10:52	11:52
8:29	---	---	9:17	---	9:54	10:54	11:54	12:54	1:54	2:54	3:54	4:36	---	5:09	---	5:39	5:54	6:54	7:54	8:54	9:54	10:54	11:54
8:30	---	---	9:18	---	---	---	---	---	---	---	---	---	---	5:11	---	5:41	---	---	---	---	---	---	---
8:35	---	---	9:23	---	9:59	10:59	11:59	12:59	1:59	2:59	3:59	4:41	4:53	5:16	5:23	5:46	5:59	6:59	7:59	8:59	9:59	10:59	11:59
8:40	---	---	9:28	---	10:04	11:04	12:04	1:04	2:04	3:04	4:04	4:46	4:58	5:21	5:28	5:51	6:04	7:04	8:04	9:04	10:04	11:04	12:04
8:43	---	---	9:31	---	10:07	11:07	12:07	1:07	2:07	3:07	4:07	4:50	5:02	5:25	5:32	5:55	6:07	7:07	8:07	9:07	10:07	11:07	12:07
8:52	8:56	9:00	9:40	9:30	10:16	11:16	12:16	1:16	2:16	3:16	4:16	4:57	5:10	5:32	5:40	6:02	6:16	7:16	8:16	9:16	10:16	11:16	12:16
			5		10	10	10	10	10	10	10	10	10	10	10	10	10	10	10	10	10	10	10

1247 PM	1249 PM	1251 PM	1253 PM	1255 PM	1257 PM	1259 PM	1261 PM	1263 PM	1265 PM	1267 PM	1269 PM	1271 PM	1273 PM	1275 PM	1277 PM	1279 PM	1281 PM	1283 PM	1303 PM	1285 PM	1287 PM	1289 PM	1291 PM	1293 PM	1295 AM
4:00	4:05	4:10	4:30	4:35	4:40	4:50	5:00	5:05	5:10	5:20	5:30	5:35	5:40	6:00	6:05	6:10	6:30	6:50	7:00	7:33	8:33	9:33	10:33	11:33	12:33
---	---	4:15	---	---	4:45	---	---	---	5:15	---	---	---	5:45	---	---	6:15	---	6:55	---	7:39	8:39	9:39	10:39	11:39	12:39
---	---	4:19	---	---	4:49	---	---	---	5:19	---	---	---	5:49	---	---	6:19	---	6:59	---	7:43	8:43	9:43	10:43	11:43	12:43
---	---	4:24	---	---	4:54	---	---	---	5:24	---	---	---	5:54	---	---	6:24	---	7:04	---	7:48	8:48	9:48	10:48	11:48	12:48
---	---	4:28	---	---	4:58	---	---	---	5:28	---	---	---	5:58	---	---	6:28	---	7:08	---	---	---	---	---	---	---
---	---	4:30	---	---	5:00	---	---	---	5:30	---	---	---	6:00	---	---	6:30	---	7:10	---	7:53	8:53	9:53	10:53	11:53	12:53
---	---	4:32	---	---	5:02	---	---	---	5:32	---	---	---	6:02	---	---	6:32	---	7:12	---	7:55	8:55	9:55	10:55	11:55	12:55
---	---	4:34	---	---	5:04	---	---	---	5:34	---	---	---	6:04	---	---	6:34	---	7:14	---	7:57	8:57	9:57	10:57	11:57	12:57
---	---	4:37	---	---	5:07	---	---	---	5:37	---	---	---	6:07	---	---	6:37	---	7:17	---	---	---	---	---	---	---
---	---	4:39	---	---	5:10	---	---	---	5:39	---	---	---	6:10	---	---	6:39	---	7:19	---	8:00	9:00	10:00	11:00	12:00	1:00
---	4:22	4:41	---	4:52	---	---	5:22	5:41	---	---	---	5:52	---	---	6:22	6:41	---	7:21	---	8:04	9:04	10:04	11:04	12:04	1:04
---	4:25	4:43	---	4:55	---	---	5:25	5:43	---	---	---	5:55	---	---	6:25	6:43	---	7:23	---	8:08	9:08	10:08	11:08	12:08	1:08
---	4:27	4:45	---	4:57	---	---	5:27	5:45	---	---	---	5:57	---	---	6:27	6:45	---	7:25	---	8:11	9:11	10:11	11:11	12:11	1:11
---	4:30	4:48	---	5:00	---	---	5:30	5:48	---	---	---	6:00	---	---	6:30	6:48	---	7:28	---	8:15	9:15	10:15	11:15	12:15	1:15
---	4:33	4:51	---	5:03	---	---	5:33	5:51	---	---	---	6:03	---	---	6:33	6:51	---	7:31	---	8:18	9:18	10:18	11:18	12:18	1:18
---	4:35	4:53	---	5:05	---	---	5:35	5:53	---	---	---	6:05	---	---	6:35	6:53	---	7:33	---	---	---	---	---	---	---
---	4:38	4:56	---	5:08	---	---	5:38	5:56	---	---	---	6:08	---	---	6:38	6:56	---	7:36	---	---	---	---	---	---	---
---	4:40	4:58	---	5:10	---	---	5:40	5:58	---	---	---	6:10	---	---	6:40	6:58	---	7:38	---	---	---	---	---	---	---
---	4:43	5:01	---	5:13	---	---	5:43	6:01	---	---	---	6:13	---	---	6:43	7:01	---	7:41	---	---	---	---	---	---	---
---	4:47	5:04	---	5:17	---	---	5:45	6:04	---	---	---	6:15	---	---	6:45	7:04	---	7:44	---	---	---	---	---	---	---
4:26	---	5:06	4:56	---	---	5:26	---	6:06	---	5:56	---	6:26	---	7:06	---	---	6:56	7:26	7:46	8:22	9:22	10:22	11:22	12:22	1:22
4:30	---	5:09	5:00	---	---	5:30	---	6:09	---	6:00	---	6:30	---	7:09	---	---	7:00	7:30	7:49	8:25	9:25	10:25	11:25	12:25	1:25
4:33	---	5:12	5:03	---	---	5:33	5:51	6:12	---	6:03	6:21	6:33	---	7:12	---	---	7:03	7:33	7:52	8:28	9:28	10:28	11:28	12:28	1:28
4:38	---	5:18	5:08	5:25	---	5:38	5:59	6:18	5:55	6:08	6:29	6:38	---	7:18	---	---	7:08	7:38	7:58	8:34	9:34	10:34	11:34	12:34	1:34
4:43	---	5:23	5:13	5:31	---	5:43	---	6:23	6:01	6:13	---	6:43	---	7:23	---	---	7:13	7:43	8:03	8:38	9:38	10:38	11:38	12:38	1:38
4:57	---	5:35	5:27	5:43	---	5:57	---	6:35	6:13	6:27	---	6:57	---	7:35	---	---	7:27	7:57	8:15	8:50	9:50	10:50	11:50	12:50	1:50
																				10	10	10	10	10	10

...ject to delays up to 10 minutes due to construction.

The top portion of the schedule shows a continuation of the Metra BNSF March 28, 2022 Monday through Friday Aurora to Chicago final morning rush-hour trips plus afternoon and evening trips. The bottom portion of the schedule shows a continuation of the Chicago to Aurora Monday through Friday afternoon rush hour service and evening service. Pages 96 and 97 taken together show that there are over thirty trains in each direction between Chicago and Aurora plus trains that cover only a portion of the line.

AURORA to CHICAGO – Saturday

	Zone	Station / Train #	2000 AM	2002 AM	2004 AM	2006 AM	2008 AM	2010 AM	2012 AM	2014 AM	2016 PM	2018 PM	2020 PM	2022 PM	2024 PM	2026 PM	2028 PM
●	H	Aurora LV	5:10	6:20	7:20	8:20	9:10	9:20	10:20	11:20	12:20	2:20	3:20	4:20	6:20	8:20	11:20
●	G	Route 59	5:18	6:28	7:28	8:28	9:20	9:28	10:28	11:28	12:28	2:28	3:30	4:28	6:28	8:28	11:28
●	F	Naperville	5:23	6:33	7:33	8:33	9:25	9:33	10:33	11:33	12:33	2:33	3:35	4:33	6:33	8:33	11:33
●	E	Lisle	5:28	6:38	7:38	8:38	9:31	9:38	10:38	11:38	12:38	2:38	3:41	4:38	6:38	8:38	11:38
●	E	Belmont	5:32	6:42	7:42	8:42	9:35	9:42	10:42	11:42	12:42	2:42	3:45	4:42	6:42	8:42	11:42
●	E	Downers Grv./Main St.	5:35	6:45	7:45	8:45	9:40	9:45	10:45	11:45	12:45	2:45	3:50	4:45	6:45	8:45	11:45
●	E	Fairview Ave.	---	6:47	7:47	8:47	---	9:47	10:47	11:47	12:47	2:47	---	4:47	6:47	8:47	11:47
●	D	Westmont	5:38	6:49	7:49	8:49	---	9:49	10:49	11:49	12:49	2:49	---	4:49	6:49	8:49	11:49
○	D	Clarendon Hills	5:41	6:52	7:52	8:52	---	9:52	10:52	11:52	12:52	2:52	---	4:52	6:52	8:52	11:51
●	D	West Hinsdale	---	---	---	---	---	---	---	---	---	---	---	---	---	---	---
●	D	Hinsdale	5:44	6:55	7:55	8:55	---	9:55	10:55	11:55	12:55	2:55	---	4:55	6:55	8:55	11:54
●	D	Highlands	---	---	---	---	---	---	---	---	---	---	---	---	---	---	---
●	D	Western Springs	5:47	6:58	7:58	8:58	---	9:58	10:58	11:58	12:58	2:58	---	4:58	6:58	8:58	11:57
●	C	LaGrange, Stone Ave.	---	7:01	8:01	9:01	---	10:01	11:01	12:01	1:01	3:01	---	5:01	7:01	9:01	---
●	C	LaGrange Rd.	5:51	7:03	8:03	9:03	---	10:03	11:03	12:03	1:03	3:03	---	5:03	7:03	9:03	12:01
	C	Congress Park	---	---	---	---	---	---	---	---	---	---	---	---	---	---	---
○	C	Brookfield	5:54	7:06	8:06	9:06	---	10:06	11:06	12:06	1:06	3:06	---	5:06	7:06	9:06	12:03
●	C	Hollywood (Zoo Stop)	---	---	---	9:08	---	10:08	11:08	12:08	1:08	3:08	---	5:08	7:08	---	---
○	C	Riverside	5:57	7:09	8:09	9:10	---	10:10	11:10	12:10	1:10	3:10	---	5:10	7:10	9:09	12:05
●	B	Harlem Ave.	---	7:11	8:11	9:12	---	10:12	11:12	12:12	1:12	3:12	---	5:12	7:12	9:11	---
●	B	Berwyn	6:00	7:13	8:13	9:14	---	10:14	11:14	12:14	1:14	3:14	---	5:14	7:14	9:13	12:08
●	B	LaVergne	---	---	---	---	---	---	---	---	---	---	---	---	---	---	---
●	B	Cicero	6:05	7:18	8:18	9:19	---	10:19	11:19	12:19	1:19	3:19	---	5:19	7:19	9:18	12:11
	A	Western Ave.	---	7:23	8:23	9:24	---	10:24	11:24	12:24	1:24	3:24	---	5:24	7:24	9:23	---
	A	Halsted St.	---	---	---	---	---	---	---	---	---	---	---	---	---	---	---
●	A	Chicago CUS AR	6:21	7:40	8:40	9:47	10:13	10:47	11:47	12:47	1:47	3:47	4:23	5:47	7:47	9:40	12:29
		# of bikes allowed per train	10	10	10	10	10	10	10	10	10	10	10	10	10	10	10
		▲ subject to construction				▲	▲	▲	▲	▲	▲	▲	▲				

CHICAGO to AURORA – Saturday

	Zone	Station / Train #	2001 AM	2003 AM	2005 AM	2007 AM	2009 PM	2011 PM	2013 PM	2015 PM	2017 PM	2019 PM	2021 PM	2023 PM	2025 PM	2027 PM	2029 AM
●	A	Chicago CUS LV	6:30	8:40	10:40	11:40	12:40	1:40	2:40	3:40	4:40	5:35	5:40	6:40	8:40	10:40	12:40
	A	Halsted St.	---	---	---	---	---	---	---	---	---	---	---	---	---	---	---
	A	Western Ave.	6:36	8:46	10:46	11:46	12:46	1:46	2:46	3:46	4:46	---	---	6:46	8:46	---	---
●	B	Cicero	6:41	8:51	10:51	11:51	12:51	1:51	2:51	3:51	4:51	---	5:51	6:51	8:51	10:51	12:51
●	B	LaVergne	---	---	---	---	---	---	---	---	---	---	---	---	---	---	---
●	B	Berwyn	6:45	8:55	10:55	11:55	12:55	1:55	2:55	3:55	4:55	---	5:55	6:55	8:55	10:55	12:55
●	B	Harlem Ave.	6:47	8:57	10:57	11:57	12:57	1:57	2:57	3:57	4:57	---	5:57	6:57	8:57	10:57	12:57
○	C	Riverside	6:49	8:59	10:59	11:59	12:59	1:59	2:59	3:59	4:59	---	5:59	6:59	8:59	10:59	12:59
●	C	Hollywood (Zoo Stop)	---	9:01	11:01	12:01	1:01	2:01	3:01	4:01	5:01	---	6:01	7:01	---	---	---
○	C	Brookfield	6:52	9:03	11:03	12:03	1:03	2:03	3:03	4:03	5:03	---	6:03	7:03	9:02	11:02	1:02
	C	Congress Park	---	---	---	---	---	---	---	---	---	---	---	---	---	---	---
●	C	LaGrange Rd.	6:55	9:06	11:06	12:06	1:06	2:06	3:06	4:06	5:06	---	6:06	7:06	9:06	11:06	1:06
●	C	LaGrange, Stone Ave.	6:57	9:08	11:08	12:08	1:08	2:08	3:08	4:08	5:08	---	6:08	7:08	9:08	11:08	1:08
●	D	Western Springs	7:00	9:11	11:11	12:11	1:11	2:11	3:11	4:11	5:11	---	6:11	7:11	9:11	11:11	1:11
●	D	Highlands	---	---	---	---	---	---	---	---	---	---	---	---	---	---	---
●	D	Hinsdale	7:03	9:14	11:14	12:14	1:14	2:14	3:14	4:14	5:14	---	6:14	7:14	9:14	11:14	1:14
●	D	West Hinsdale	---	---	---	---	---	---	---	---	---	---	---	---	---	---	---
○	D	Clarendon Hills	7:06	9:17	11:17	12:17	1:17	2:17	3:17	4:17	5:17	---	6:17	7:17	9:17	11:17	1:17
●	D	Westmont	7:09	9:20	11:20	12:20	1:20	2:20	3:20	4:20	5:20	---	6:20	7:20	9:20	11:20	1:20
●	E	Fairview Ave.	7:12	9:23	11:23	12:23	1:23	2:23	3:23	4:23	5:23	---	6:23	7:23	9:23	11:23	1:23
●	E	Downers Grv./Main St	7:14	9:25	11:25	12:25	1:25	2:25	3:25	4:25	5:25	5:59	6:25	7:25	9:25	11:25	1:25
●	E	Belmont	7:17	9:28	11:28	12:28	1:28	2:28	3:28	4:28	5:28	6:03	6:28	7:28	9:28	11:28	1:28
●	E	Lisle	7:20	9:31	11:31	12:31	1:31	2:31	3:31	4:31	5:31	6:07	6:31	7:31	9:31	11:31	1:31
●	F	Naperville	7:26	9:37	11:37	12:37	1:37	2:37	3:37	4:37	5:37	6:13	6:37	7:37	9:37	11:37	1:37
●	G	Route 59	7:31	9:42	11:42	12:42	1:42	2:42	3:42	4:42	5:42	6:18	6:42	7:42	9:42	11:42	1:42
●	H	Aurora AR	7:45	10:01	12:01	1:01	2:01	3:01	4:01	5:01	6:01	6:31	7:01	8:01	10:00	12:00	1:56
		# of bikes allowed per train	10	10	10	10	10	10	10	10	10	10	10	10	10	10	10
		▲ subject to construction		▲	▲	▲	▲	▲	▲	▲							

ᕦ = ADA Accessibility: ● = ADA Accessible Station   O = Partially ADA Accessible Station – station meets some, but not all ADA requirements. | ∗ = Sunday sched[e]

The Metra BNSF Aurora–Chicago March 28, 2022 Saturday schedule shows there are fifteen trains in each direction. Saturday service from Aurora to Chicago was generally hourly except for an additional 9:10 a.m. train from Aurora that is local to Downers Grove and then express to Chicago plus a 5:35 p.m. express train from Chicago to Downers Grove and then local to Aurora.

AURORA to CHICAGO – Sunday/Holiday*

ADA	Zone	Train # Station	2002 AM	2006 AM	2010 AM	2012 AM	2016 PM	2018 PM	2022 PM	2024 PM	2026 PM	2028 PM
●	H	Aurora LV:	6:20	8:20	9:20	10:20	12:20	2:20	4:20	6:20	8:20	11:20
●	G	Route 59	6:28	8:28	9:28	10:28	12:28	2:28	4:28	6:28	8:28	11:28
●	F	Naperville	6:33	8:33	9:33	10:33	12:33	2:33	4:33	6:33	8:33	11:33
●	E	Lisle	6:38	8:38	9:38	10:38	12:38	2:38	4:38	6:38	8:38	11:38
●	E	Belmont	6:42	8:42	9:42	10:42	12:42	2:42	4:42	6:42	8:42	11:42
●	E	Downers Grv./Main St.	6:45	8:45	9:45	10:45	12:45	2:45	4:45	6:45	8:45	11:45
●	E	Fairview Ave.	6:47	8:47	9:47	10:47	12:47	2:47	4:47	6:47	8:47	11:47
●	D	Westmont	6:49	8:49	9:49	10:49	12:49	2:49	4:49	6:49	8:49	11:49
○	D	Clarendon Hills	6:52	8:52	9:52	10:52	12:52	2:52	4:52	6:52	8:52	11:51
●	D	West Hinsdale	---	---	---	---	---	---	---	---	---	---
●	D	Hinsdale	6:55	8:55	9:55	10:55	12:55	2:55	4:55	6:55	8:55	11:54
●	D	Highlands	---	---	---	---	---	---	---	---	---	---
●	D	Western Springs	6:58	8:58	9:58	10:58	12:58	2:58	4:58	6:58	8:58	11:57
●	C	LaGrange, Stone Ave.	7:01	9:01	10:01	11:01	1:01	3:01	5:01	7:01	9:01	---
●	C	LaGrange Rd.	7:03	9:03	10:03	11:03	1:03	3:03	5:03	7:03	9:03	12:01
	C	Congress Park	---	---	---	---	---	---	---	---	---	---
○	C	Brookfield	7:06	9:06	10:06	11:06	1:06	3:06	5:06	7:06	9:06	12:03
●	C	Hollywood (Zoo Stop)	---	9:08	10:08	11:08	1:08	3:08	5:08	7:08	---	---
○	C	Riverside	7:09	9:10	10:10	11:10	1:10	3:10	5:10	7:10	9:09	12:05
●	B	Harlem Ave.	7:11	9:12	10:12	11:12	1:12	3:12	5:12	7:12	9:11	---
●	B	Berwyn	7:13	9:14	10:14	11:14	1:14	3:14	5:14	7:14	9:13	12:08
●	B	LaVergne	---	---	---	---	---	---	---	---	---	---
●	B	Cicero	7:18	9:19	10:19	11:19	1:19	3:19	5:19	7:19	9:18	12:11
	A	Western Ave.	7:23	9:24	10:24	11:24	1:24	3:24	5:24	7:24	9:23	---
	A	Halsted St.	---	---	---	---	---	---	---	---	---	---
●	A	Chicago CUS AR:	7:40	9:47	10:47	11:47	1:47	3:47	5:47	7:47	9:40	12:29
🚲		# of bikes allowed per train	10	10	10	10	10	10	10	10	10	10
▲		subject to construction		▲	▲	▲	▲	▲				

CHICAGO to AURORA – Sunday/Holiday*

ADA	Zone	Train # Station	2003 AM	2005 AM	2009 PM	2013 PM	2017 PM	2021 PM	2023 PM	2025 PM	2027 PM	2029 AM
●	A	Chicago CUS LV:	8:40	10:40	12:40	2:40	4:40	5:40	6:40	8:40	10:40	12:40
	A	Halsted St.	---	---	---	---	---	---	---	---	---	---
	A	Western Ave.	8:46	10:46	12:46	2:46	4:46	---	6:46	8:46	---	---
●	B	Cicero	8:51	10:51	12:51	2:51	4:51	5:51	6:51	8:51	10:51	12:51
●	B	LaVergne	---	---	---	---	---	---	---	---	---	---
●	B	Berwyn	8:55	10:55	12:55	2:55	4:55	5:55	6:55	8:55	10:55	12:55
●	B	Harlem Ave.	8:57	10:57	12:57	2:57	4:57	5:57	6:57	8:57	10:57	12:57
○	C	Riverside	8:59	10:59	12:59	2:59	4:59	5:59	6:59	8:59	10:59	12:59
●	C	Hollywood (Zoo Stop)	9:01	11:01	1:01	3:01	5:01	6:01	7:01	---	---	---
○	C	Brookfield	9:03	11:03	1:03	3:03	5:03	6:03	7:03	9:02	11:02	1:02
	C	Congress Park	---	---	---	---	---	---	---	---	---	---
●	C	LaGrange Rd.	9:06	11:06	1:06	3:06	5:06	6:06	7:06	9:06	11:06	1:06
●	C	LaGrange, Stone Ave.	9:08	11:08	1:08	3:08	5:08	6:08	7:08	9:08	11:08	1:08
●	D	Western Springs	9:11	11:11	1:11	3:11	5:11	6:11	7:11	9:11	11:11	1:11
●	D	Highlands	---	---	---	---	---	---	---	---	---	---
●	D	Hinsdale	9:14	11:14	1:14	3:14	5:14	6:14	7:14	9:14	11:14	1:14
●	D	West Hinsdale	---	---	---	---	---	---	---	---	---	---
○	D	Clarendon Hills	9:17	11:17	1:17	3:17	5:17	6:17	7:17	9:17	11:17	1:17
●	D	Westmont	9:20	11:20	1:20	3:20	5:20	6:20	7:20	9:20	11:20	1:20
●	E	Fairview Ave.	9:23	11:23	1:23	3:23	5:23	6:23	7:23	9:23	11:23	1:23
●	E	Downers Grv./Main St	9:25	11:25	1:25	3:25	5:25	6:25	7:25	9:25	11:25	1:25
●	E	Belmont	9:28	11:28	1:28	3:28	5:28	6:28	7:28	9:28	11:28	1:28
●	E	Lisle	9:31	11:31	1:31	3:31	5:31	6:31	7:31	9:31	11:31	1:31
●	F	Naperville	9:37	11:37	1:37	3:37	5:37	6:37	7:37	9:37	11:37	1:37
●	G	Route 59	9:42	11:42	1:42	3:42	5:42	6:42	7:42	9:42	11:42	1:42
●	H	Aurora AR:	10:01	12:01	2:01	4:01	6:01	7:01	8:01	10:00	12:00	1:56
🚲		# of bikes allowed per train	10	10	10	10	10	10	10	10	10	10
▲		subject to construction	▲	▲	▲	▲						

♿ = ADA Accessibility: ● = ADA Accessible

The March 28, 2022 Metra BNSF Sunday/Holiday Metra schedule shows there are ten trains every two hours in each direction on the Aurora–Chicago line. On Saturday, Sunday, and major holidays, no passenger trains stop at Halsted St., LaVergne, Congress Park, Highlands, and West Hinsdale.

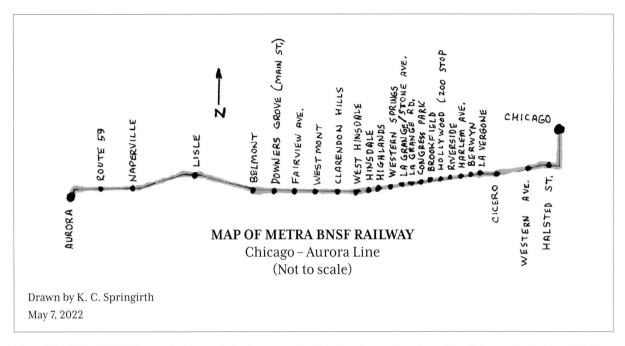

Map of the Metra BNSF Chicago to Aurora, Illinois, commuter line showing station stops. The Chicago, Burlington & Quincy Railroad heritage resulted in an efficient and well-equipped rail commuter service.

Amtrak four-axle 3,000-horsepower diesel electric locomotive No. 90215 type F40PH (built by EMD in April 1976) is at the Metra BNSF station located at 914 Burlington Avenue in the village of Western Springs in Cook County, Illinois on May 25, 2008. This suburb of Chicago has grown in population from 6,364 in 1950 to 13,629 in 2020. (*Kenneth C. Springirth photograph*)

The Metra BNSF station at 1 South Prospect Avenue in Clarendon Hills, DuPage County, Illinois, is the location for Metra 3,200 horsepower locomotive No. 192 (type F40PHM-2 built by EMD in February 1992) heading a train making a station stop on May 27, 2008. Clarendon Hills (a village in DuPage County, Illinois, and southwestern suburb of Chicago) has grown in population from 2,437 in 1950 to 8,702 in 2020. (*Kenneth C. Springirth photograph*)

On May 26, 2008, at the Clarendon Hills station, a Metra BNSF commuter train powered by 3,600-horsepower locomotive No. 403 (type MP36PH-3S built by Motive Power Industries in 2003) is waiting for the signal to depart. (*Kenneth C. Springirth photograph*)

Two Metra BNSF commuter trains are side by side headed (*from left to right*) by locomotives No. 403 (type MP36PH-3S built by Motive Power Industries in 2003) and No. 205 (EMD F40PHM-2 built in August 1992) are at the Clarendon Hills station on May 27, 2008. (*Kenneth C. Springirth photograph*)

A Metra BNSF commuter train led by locomotive No. 404 (type MP36PH-3S built by Motive Power Industries in March 2003) is ready to depart from Western Springs, Illinois, on May 26, 2008. (*Kenneth C. Springirth photograph*)

Streamlined Metra BNSF locomotive No. 405 (type MP36PH-3S built in May 26, 2003) is ready to proceed with its train of double-decker commuter coaches at Western Springs, Illinois, on March 26, 2008. (*Kenneth C. Springirth photograph*)

This is an end view of a Metra BNSF control car at the end of the commuter train at Western Springs, Illinois, on May 26, 2008. Developed during 1964–1965, a control car has all of the controls and gauges to remotely operate the locomotive and enables a push pull operation when located at the end of a train which has the locomotive at the opposite end of the train. Hence the train can be manned from either the engine in one direction, or from the last car in the other direction. This enables the train to reverse direction without having to turn around. (*Kenneth C. Springirth photograph*)

In addition to Metra BNSF commuter rail service, these tracks at Western Springs, Illinois, host BNSF freight trains as evidenced by BNSF No. 6109 (GE ES44AC built in September 2006) the trailing locomotive on a coal train passing by the Western Springs, Illinois, train station on May 26, 2008. (*Kenneth C. Springirth photograph*)

On April 28, 2022, an eastbound Metra BNSF commuter train, with locomotive No. 185 (EMD F40PHM-2 built in October 1991) at the rear of the train, is leaving Naperville, Illinois. Ridership has decreased on the BNSF (Chicago–Aurora) line (which has the largest ridership of the eleven Metra lines) from 16,658,357 in 2014 to 15,468,014 in 2019; however, as result of the COVID-19 epidemic, it decreased to 3,659,617 in 2020. Metra's total eleven-line ridership decreased from 83,369,706 in 2014 to 74,043,516 in 2019 and to 18,611,311 in 2020 because of the COVID-19 epidemic. (*Kenneth C. Springirth photograph*)

On April 28, 2022, the westbound Amtrak *California Zephyr* headed by 4,250-horsepower locomotive No. 33 (GE P42DC built in December 1996) is preparing to leave the Naperville, Illinois, station for its trip via Omaha, Nebraska; and Salt Lake City, Utah, to the San Francisco Bay Area at Emeryville, California. (*Kenneth C. Springirth photograph*)

A westbound freight train is passing through Naperville, Illinois, on April 28, 2022 powered by BNSF locomotive No. 5018 (GE C44-9W built in August 2004) and Norfolk Southern Railway locomotive No. 4280 GE type AC44C6M (originally No. 9026 D9-44CW built in February 1997 and rebuilt and renumbered in February 2020 at the Norfolk Southern Juniata Locomotive Shop) via this three track mainline called the raceway. (*Kenneth C. Springirth photograph*)

On 105 E. Fourth Avenue in the city of Naperville, Illinois, at the Metra BNSF station is the location on April 28, 2022 of westbound Metra BNSF commuter train headed by locomotive No. 210 (EMD F40PHM-2 built in October 1992). (*Kenneth C. Springirth photograph*)

On April 28, 2022, a bicycle car is on a westbound Metra BNSF commuter train viewed at the Naperville, Illinois, train station. Metra introduced bicycle cars in November 2020. The bicycle car has racks for sixteen bicycles and can be spotted by its special blue paint scheme with a horizontal red line near the car bottom with a white bicycle decal next to the outside doors. To accommodate bicycles, twenty-four two-passenger seats were removed on one half of the lower level. Seats remain on the upper level of that side of the car for passengers who want to sit within view of their bike. (*Kenneth C. Springirth photograph*)

An eastbound Metra BNSF commuter train with rear locomotive No. 200 (EMD F40PHM-2 built in May 1992) is pushing away from the Naperville, Illinois, station platform on April 28, 2022 passing a springtime scene of white blossoms on a line of trees parallel to the track. (*Kenneth C. Springirth photograph*)

The westbound Amtrak Southwest Chief, heading for Los Angeles, California, powered by locomotives No. 23 (GE P42DC built in November 1996) and No. 137 (GE P42DC built in January 2001) is at a station stop at Naperville, Illinois, on April 28, 2022. In addition to the westbound and eastbound Southwest Chief, Naperville is also served by the eastbound and westbound *California Zephyr*, the eastbound and westbound *Illinois Zephyr*, and the eastbound and westbound *Carl Sandburg*. Hence eight Amtrak trains stop at Naperville. (*Kenneth C. Springirth photograph*)

Metra BNSF commuter train powered by locomotive No. 204 (EMD F40PHM-2 built in August 1992) is making a station stop at Naperville, Illinois, on April 28, 2022. (*Kenneth C. Springirth photograph*)

On a cloudy bright April 28, 2022, a westbound BNSF intermodal train powered by three BNSF locomotives headed by No. 6135 (GE ES44AC built in November 2006) is passing by the Metra BNSF Naperville, Illinois, station. This long train came through about fifteen minutes ahead of the next scheduled westbound Metra BNSF commuter train. On the same track, the Metra BNSF commuter train arrived at the station on time. Metra, Amtrak, and BNSF Railway do an excellent job maintaining schedules on a very busy rail line. (*Kenneth C. Springirth photograph*)

On the rear of the above April 28, 2022 westbound intermodal train BNSF locomotive No. 4762 (GE C44-9W built in May 1998) is passing by the Metra BNSF Naperville, Illinois, station. (*Kenneth C. Springirth photograph*)

On April 28, 2022, Metra BNSF locomotive No. 180 (EMD F40PH-2 built in March 1989) is ready to leave Naperville, Illinois, for the eastbound commuter train trip to Chicago. (*Kenneth C. Springirth photograph*)

From left to right: westbound commuter train headed by Metra BNSF locomotive No. 199 (EMD F40PHM-2 built in May 1992) and eastbound commuter train pushed by Metra BNSF locomotive No. 204 (EMD F40PHM-2 built in August 1992) on April 28, 2022 have met at Naperville, Illinois, train station. (*Kenneth C. Springirth photograph*)

Metra BNSF locomotive No. 210 (EMD F40PHM-2 built in October 1992) is eastbound leaving the Naperville, Illinois, train station on April 28, 2022. (*Kenneth C. Springirth photograph*)

On April 28, 2022, Metra BNSF locomotive No. 185 (EMD FG40PHM-2 built in October 1991) is eastbound preparing to leave the Naperville, Illinois, train station. (*Kenneth C. Springirth photograph*)

A commuter train is at the 1000 Front Street train station in the village of Lisle in DuPage County, Illinois, on April 29, 2022 ready to be pushed eastbound to Chicago by Metra BNSF locomotive No. 204 (EMD F40PHM-2 built in August 1992). The population of Lisle increased from 4,219 in 1960 to 24,223 in 2020. A number of companies have relocated to Lisle seeking an easily accessible, highly visible alternative to Chicago. (*Kenneth C. Springirth photograph*)

A westbound commuter train is pulling into Lisle, Illinois, powered by Metra BNSF locomotive No. 199 (EMD F40PHM-2 built in May 1992) on a cloudy April 29, 2022. (*Kenneth C. Springirth photograph*)

On April 29, 2022, the Aurora, Illinois, Transportation Center is the location of well-maintained former Chicago, Burlington & Quincy Railroad wide vision caboose No. 13690. Modern freight railroads have replaced the caboose with an end of train device which is a relatively small box attached to the end of the last car. The paperwork, which the crew once did regarding freight cars, loads, maintenance concerns, and trip logging, is now automated and computerized. Cabooses are now only used in special situations such as where a train must be backed up or for transportation of maintenance crews. (*Kenneth C. Springirth photograph*)

Metra BNSF commuter train powered by locomotive No. 206 is getting ready for departure time from the Aurora, Illinois, Transportation Center for the next trip to Chicago on April 29, 2022. This facility, located at 233 N. Broadway at Aurora, Illinois, opened in 1988 replacing the former station which was constructed in 1922 by the Chicago, Burlington & Quincy Railroad at South Broadway and Washington Street in downtown Aurora. That station (also serving Amtrak and Metra trains) was torn down in April 2013. When the new station opened at the former Chicago, Burlington & Quincy Aurora Roundhouse and shops, it had a sub end terminus for Metra commuter train service, increased parking capacity, and Amtrak trains were shifted to Naperville, Illinois. (*Kenneth C. Springirth photograph*)

On April 29, 2022, westbound Metra BNSF commuter train, powered by Locomotive No. 117 (rebuilt EMD F40PH-3 originally built in October 1977) and No. 189 (EMD F40PHM-2 built in December 1991) is at the village of Downers Grove, a southeastern suburb of Chicago, in DuPage County, Illinois, on April 29, 2022. Downers Grove population increased from 10,886 in 1950 to 50,247 in 2020. However, there was a 1.8 percent population loss from 48,724 in 2000 to 47,833 in 2010. Many residents commute via Metra to Chicago; however, Downers Grove has many businesses and offices of national corporations.

An eastbound BNSF general manifest train is passing through scenic Downers Grove on April 29, 2022 headed by locomotive No. 4180 (GE C44-9W built in June 2002). (*Kenneth C. Springirth photograph*)

A BNSF general manifest train on April 29, 2022 is passing through Lisle, Illinois, powered by locomotive No. 5854 (GE ES44AC built in January 2006). (*Kenneth C. Springirth photograph*)

On April 29, 2022, Metra BNSF locomotive No. 204 (EMD F40PHM-2 built in August 1992) is leaving the 5001 Main Street train station in the village of Downers Grove, DuPage County, Illinois, on an eastbound commuter train trip to Chicago. (*Kenneth C. Springirth photograph*)

A westbound BNSF freight train on April 29, 2022 is passing by the Downers Grove, Illinois, passenger station powered by locomotive No. 5004 (GE C44-9W built in August 2004). (*Kenneth C. Springirth photograph*)

On April 29, 2022, Metra BNSF locomotive No. 117 (rebuilt EMD F40PH-3 originally F40PH built in October 1977) is at the village of Hinsdale in Cook and DuPage counties, Illinois. This historic station, originally known as the Brush Hill Train Station was designed for the Chicago, Burlington & Quincy Railroad by architect Walter T. Kraush, built by Grace & Hyde Company in 1899, and is part of the downtown Hinsdale Historic District. (*Kenneth C. Springirth photograph*)

A westbound Amtrak train powered by locomotive No. 54 (GE P42DC built in January 1997) is passing by the Hinsdale, Illinois, station on April 29, 2022. Hinsdale has increased in population from 8,676 in 1950 to 17,395 in 2020. However, there was a 4.2 percent decline in population from 16,726 in 1980 to 16,029 in 1990 plus a 3.1 percent decline in population from 17,349 in 2000 to 16,816 in 2010. While many Hinsdale residents commute to jobs in the Chicago, Hinsdale has many small- and medium-sized businesses. (*Kenneth C. Springirth photograph*)

On April 29, 2022, Canadian Pacific Railway locomotives headed by No. 8700 (GE ES44AC built in November 2005) are powering an intermodal train passing the 21 East Hinsdale Avenue Metra BNSF train station in the village of Hinsdale, Illinois. (*Kenneth C. Springirth photograph*)

An eastbound BNSF freight train is passing by the Hinsdale, Illinois, station on April 29, 2022 powered by locomotive No. 5312 (GE C44-9W built in June 2001). Since this commuter line sees many freight trains, it is important for passengers waiting for their next train to keep a safe distance from the train track. (*Kenneth C. Springirth photograph*)

On April 29, 2022, a BNSF eastbound intermodal train headed by locomotive No. 4345 (GE C44-9W built in February 1999) is on the middle track and will shortly be past the Hinsdale, Illinois, station. (*Kenneth C. Springirth photograph*)

An afternoon fast-moving Amtrak train on April 29, 2022 headed by locomotive No. 167 (GE P42DC built May 2001) is express through Hinsdale, Illinois. (*Kenneth C. Springirth photograph*)

Passengers at the Hinsdale, Illinois, station are boarding Metra BNSF commuter cars on April 29, 2022 for their eastbound trip to Chicago pushed by locomotive No. 194 (EMD F40PHM-2 built in March 1992). (*Kenneth C. Springirth photograph*)

On April 29, 2022, a westbound BNSF intermodal train powered by locomotive No. 4148 (GE C44-9W built in September 2002) is efficiently making its way past the Hinsdale, Illinois, station. (*Kenneth C. Springirth photograph*)

On a quiet Saturday morning April 30, 2022 at the Naperville, Illinois, train station, eastbound Metra BNSF locomotive No. 195 (EMD F40PHM-2 built in March 1992) is about to push the eastbound commuter train to Chicago. (*Kenneth C. Springirth photograph*)

Amid a light rainy April 30, 2022 Saturday morning, the eastbound Amtrak *Illinois Zephyr* powered by locomotive No. 4625 (Siemens SC-44 which stands for Siemens Charger 4,400 horsepower and was designed and manufactured by Siemens Mobility in September 2017 for Amtrak state-supported inter-city service) is pulling into the Naperville, Illinois, station. Note on the side of the locomotive near the front shows the reporting mark IDTX (which stands for Illinois Department of Transportation) and the locomotive No. 4625. This is the morning train from Quincy, Illinois, to Chicago, Illinois. It leaves Chicago early evening for the trip back to Quincy. There is also an afternoon train known as the Carl Sandburg that leaves Chicago in the morning for Quincy, Illinois, and leaves Quincy in the afternoon for the trip back to Chicago. Both of these trains receive funding from the State of Illinois. (*Kenneth C. Springirth photograph*)

On a rainy April 30, 2022, BNSF locomotive No. 5312 (GE C44-9W built in June 2001) is heading an eastbound freight train past the Naperville, Illinois, train station. One day earlier as shown on page 117, this same locomotive was handling a train at Hinsdale, Illinois. (*Kenneth C. Springirth photograph*)

Eastbound Metra BNSF commuter train locomotive No. 181 (EMD F40PH-2 built in July 1989) is leaving the Naperville, Illinois, train station for a Saturday morning trip to Chicago on April 30, 2022. (*Kenneth C. Springirth photograph*)

On April 30, 2022, westbound Metra BNSF locomotive No. 210 (EMD F40PHM-2 is leaving the Naperville, Illinois, train station with bi-level stainless steel commuter cars built by the Budd Company). These cars became known as "Gallery" cars because the upper level was designed with the center section open so that the conductor could reach the tickets from upper-level passengers. The first thirty of these cars were delivered between August 1950 and January 1951 and were the first commuter cars to have air conditioning. Budd continued to build "Gallery" cars for the Burlington until the 1960s and for Burlington Northern until the 1970s. (*Kenneth C. Springirth photograph*)

A close-up view of Chicago Burlington & Quincy Railroad bi-level stainless-steel commuter car No. 768 built by the Budd Company in 1965 and rebuilt in 1973 with original Burlington signage on the car above center entranceway and BNSF below it next to the center entranceway of the car as the eastbound Metra BNSF commuter train receives passengers at the Naperville, Illinois, station on April 30, 2022. (*Kenneth C. Springirth photograph*)

Metra BNSF locomotive No. 183 (rebuilt EMD F40PH-3 built in September 1989) is pushing away from the Naperville, Illinois, station for an April 30, 2022 afternoon trip to Chicago. (*Kenneth C. Springirth photograph*)

On April 30, 2022, BNSF locomotive No. 7578 (GE ES44DC built June 2007) is leading with three diesel units behind it powering a westbound BNSF intermodal train passing by the Naperville, Illinois, station. (*Kenneth C. Springirth photograph*)

A general manifest train on April 30, 2022, headed by BNSF locomotive No. 4086 (GE C44-9W built in June 2003), with two units behind it, is westbound on track two of the three track main line with passengers on the platform of the Naperville, Illinois, train station waiting for the next Metra commuter train to Chicago. (*Kenneth C. Springirth photograph*)

On April 30, 2022, a fast westbound BNSF intermodal train led by locomotive No. 7034 (type GE ES44C4 built in May 2012) is on the westbound passenger track passing the Naperville, Illinois, station. (*Kenneth C. Springirth photograph*)

An eastbound BNSF coal train powered by locomotive No. 6246 (GE ES44AC built in October 2008) is coming through Naperville, Illinois, on a cloudy Saturday April 30, 2022. (*Kenneth C. Springirth photograph*)

The westbound Amtrak Southwest Chief is making a passenger stop at Naperville, Illinois, on April 30, 2022 powered by locomotives No. 167 (GE P42DC built in May 2001), No. 29 (GE P42DC built in November 1996), and No. 45 (GE P42DC built in January 1997). This is the successor to the Super Chief inaugurated by the Atchison, Topeka, and Santa Fe Railway in 1936. It was merged with the El Capitan in 1958, and became known as the Super Chief/El Capitan. Amtrak renamed it Super Chief in 1973. (*Kenneth C. Springirth photograph*)

Westbound Metra BNSF commuter train powered by locomotive No. 195 (EMD F40PHM-2 built in March 1992) on April 30, 2022 is ready to leave the Naperville, Illinois, train station for Aurora, Illinois. (*Kenneth C. Springirth photograph*)

On the morning of May 2, 2022, westbound Metra BNSF locomotive No. 192 (EMD F40PHM-2 built in February 1992) is arriving at Lisle, Illinois, for a quick stop. (*Kenneth C. Springirth photograph*)

From left to right: Metra BNSF locomotives No. 122 (rebuilt EMD F40PH-3 originally built in November 1977) and No. 182 (rebuilt EMD F40PH-3 originally built in August 1989) are pushing an eastbound commuter train into the Lisle, Illinois, station on May 2, 2022. (*Kenneth C. Springirth photograph*)

The above May 2, 2022 train, with locomotives Nos. 122 and 182, has come to a station stop at Lisle, Illinois. (*Kenneth C. Springirth photograph*)

On a cloudy bright May 2, 2022, Metra BNSF commuter train pushed by locomotive No. 208 (EMD F40PHM-2 built in October 1992) is carefully leaving the Lisle, Illinois, station eastbound for Chicago. (*Kenneth C. Springirth photograph*)

On May 2, 2022, Metra BNSF commuter train locomotive No. 192 (EMD F40PHM-2 built in February 1992) is leaving the Lisle, Illinois, station providing riders a safer and less stressful trip to Chicago than the crowded expressway. (*Kenneth C. Springirth photograph*)